The Caged Bird Finally Sings

———

Robyne Henry

Table of Contents

Acknowledgement..4

Introduction 5

Chapter 1: Rejection... 6

Chapter 2: Silence 14

Chapter 3: Abuse.. 20

Chapter 4: Denial 35

Chapter 5: The Truth... 44

Chapter 6: Broken 54

Chapter 7: Healing... 65

Chapter 8: Freedom 84

Meet the Author 105

Connect with Robyne Henry 106

Resources 107

Sources...108

Acknowledgement

Firstly, I would just like to thank my Lord and Saviour, Jesus Christ because, without Him, I am nothing. Walking on this journey as a Believer has not been easy, but He has been my Sustainer. I would like to thank my mother and my sister, Ansonia, for being there as I embarked on this new journey. Thank you Mommy for being there when I cried because life's weights were just too heavy to bear, for reassuring me of your presence and that, no matter what, you'd always be there. Thank you for always sharing a good laugh with me and pushing me forward. I love you. Thank you, Ansonia (Sone-Sone), for allowing me to crash at your place as I fought to maneuver through life while writing this book. It was not easy, but you were there and I thank you.

Thank you to my amazing best friends, Arianna and Marissa. You ladies have been my support system through it all and I cannot thank you enough. Thank you Arianna for always being a call away, and Marissa for always keeping your girl smiling. Thank you Oge, Ejiroghene, Damilare, Ayesha, and Franita; you ladies have blessed me beyond measure.

Thank you to my phenomenal spiritual leaders, Pastor Joshua and First Lady Charmecia Okpara. Writing this book has been the hardest thing I have ever done in life. The rawness of it intimidated me and made me question my purpose and calling. With all your prayers and our hour-long conversations, I was able to make it over, so I thank you.

Introduction

I have always liked to describe myself as a silent speaker—one who shares surface level things about herself but never the intimate things that haunt me. As a little girl who lived in a single parent household, I was always very quiet and to myself. Many could believe that I had it made and that I never experienced pain, but my journals spoke the truth. My journals exposed everything that my lips could never say to others and that is where all my secrets lied—in my journal.

I love my father, but he and I have a strenuous relationship, which led me to find love in all the wrong things and people. With my identity taking a hit, I became everything anyone told me to be. I stayed in relationships past their expiration dates because of the fear of having to look at myself and see my pain. I ran from freedom until it ran into me, and there was no escaping. Speaking was the only thing that was going to set me free from the chains that held me tight for so many years. In this book, I speak about my pain, my abuse, my silence and my freedom. I share how I became free and why this caged bird finally sings.

1.

Rejection

At the age of three, Mary-Ann found herself in love with a man— her father. Her mother and father were married, but her father didn't live with them. Monday through Friday, it was just Mary-Ann and her mother; Saturday's were her days with her father. On the Saturday's her father wasn't around, her mother would come up with fun activities to keep Mary-Ann busy. The two would visit the library and listen to some of R&B's finest: Otis Redding and Al Greene. After the library, they'd stop by the Sonic near their house and just listen to the music on the way home. Mary-Ann would sing Norah Jones's "Heart of Mine" with all her might. She and her mother would alternate between parts and, sometimes, sing along to it as a duet. Mary-Ann loved the time she spent with her parents. She had a different relationship with each of them, but there was a balance. She grew up around a mixed culture: her mother was from Liberia, West Africa and her father was from Saint Lucia. Because she was with her mother majority of the week, she picked up more on her African culture. She always wanted to go to her parents' homelands so she could have a deeper connection with both her parents, but especially her father.

When her father would come by, he'd sit with Mary-Ann for hours until it was time for him leave again. She always loved to see her daddy at her mother's house. Even if her parents didn't act like a family, it made her feel a little safer with him there. When it was time for him to go, she hated to see him leave. She would cry on her father's shoulder and beg him not to leave, but he'd tell her, "Babes, I gotta go." She'd stare through the gated bars of her backdoor and scream, "Daddy, I love you!" He'd turn around and look Mary-Ann in the eyes and say, "I love you too pumpkin," then he'd walk away into the darkness. She never understood why he had to leave if he loved her.

Her earliest memory was when she was almost a year old. Her father had her in the car seat and drove to his friends to show off his baby girl. She remembered hearing the excitement in her father's voice as he boasted, "This is my girl." She loved everything about her father. She loved the way he carried her on his shoulders as he ran around the backyard. He never let her fall, and even if she did, he was always there to catch her. She knew there was safety in his arms. He made her feel unstoppable and capable of anything because, if he said so, she could do it. His love for Mary-Ann was a love like no other. She was his baby girl, his princess. He complimented her whenever he saw her new hair styles or the chic clothes her mother dressed her in. Sometimes, Mary-Ann would catch him just staring at her and smiling and she'd blush. Her father gave her the best hugs. He held her close and never wanted to let her go. Often times, they'd sit in the backyard together competing with one another on who loved the other more. The winner got lunch, and Mary-Ann always won, so he'd take her to an Asian buffet. Her eyes lit up as she'd watch in amazement at the many plates her father would eat. After lunch, they'd get ice cream and bond over reggae music as the sun went down. The random neighborhood dogs barked, the birds went to their hiding places, and Mary-Ann went to the arms of her father. He was strong and invincible. Nothing could stand in the way of his love for her, or so she thought.

Mary-Ann's empire came to its ruins when her parents had gotten divorced. It didn't initially affect her because her father didn't stay at the house, but their weekend dates became strained and the drop-off fights became intense. Overwhelmed, as she witnessed both people she loved howl at each other, she would begin to cry and her mother would say, "Look what you did to her!" Her father responded, "Don't worry my girl. You know I love you." She was torn. "How do I make them stop?" she thought. She screamed, "STOP IT!" Her father shook his head and walked away. Wanting to reach him, Mary-Ann held one hand to the gated bar while her other hand was reaching for her father as she screamed, "Daddy!" But, he was already gone.

When her father left, her mother did also. Her mother had picked her up one day from school and said, "I have a friend I want you to meet." Mary-Ann was excited. Thinking it was her mother's female friend, she replied, "Okay Mommy!" The day she was supposed to meet this friend, Mary-Ann asked, "Where's your friend, Mommy?" Her mother responded, "They'll be here tomorrow, don't worry." The day had come to meet her mother's friend and there was a man walking towards her mother's car. "Who the heck is that?" she thought. The man opened the door and Mary-Ann finally met this mysterious "friend". "It's a boy!" she exclaimed to her mother. "Mommy, I thought you were only friends with girls?" Her mother shushed her and told her to behave. "Hello princess," said the man. "How are you?" Without making eye contact, she answered, "Hi, I'm fine." Who was this mysterious man and what was he doing around her mother? As the weeks turned into months, Mary-Ann noticed that she and her mother stopped going to the library. Mary-Ann would wake and try to dress herself to her best ability, then go to her mother's room and say, "Mommy, I'm ready for the library." Her mother would respond, "Not today, Pumpkin. Maybe next Saturday." Disappointed, Mary-Ann said, "Okay, Mommy." She waited patiently for next Saturday, but it never came. It continued that way until she didn't even bother to get up for her weekly library trip. The mysterious man was still there, and at this point, he was overstaying his welcome. One night, Mary-Ann's mother and the mysterious man sat her down in her room and spoke the words that shattered her glass house forever, "We're getting married." Mary-Ann broke loose from her mother's grip and screamed, "No!" The relationship she and her mother had was never the same. She viewed her as a traitor—someone who didn't value her love, so she found someone else. Her relationship with her mother was still in its developing stages; it was fragile, and when her mother got married, it damaged the relationship, leaving Mary-Ann unable to confide in her mother about how she truly felt about everything that was to come.

After the dust had settled, whenever her father was in town, she would eagerly call him and boldly say, "Daddy, come get me!" He'd respond, "Alright, prepare yourself. I'm coming!" With Lucky Dude blasting from down the street, Mary-Ann knew when her father was around. She'd expeditiously run outside to dance to the music as her father pulled up. She'd wave at him while smiling from ear to ear. "Hi Daddy!" she yelled. He'd respond, "Hello, Pumpkin," as he helped her get in the truck. When she had her seat belt buckled, he'd blast the music, rub her earlobe and smile. He'd always take her to the corner store to get chips and candy, then the two would go wherever she desired.

The moments she spent alone again with her father were moments she would cherish for a lifetime. She loved being away with her father because she didn't have the pressures of fitting into her new normal back at her mother's. Being with her father seemed never-ending. It was like it was just the two of them, Mary-Ann and her daddy. One particular Saturday, she called her father and waited for him by the backdoor. She waited hours for him, but he never came. This was the first time her father had broken a promise. After this incident, she was upset with him, but he always had a way of getting back in her good graces. It was time for their routine dates, and she did what she always did: prepared herself. When her father came, he didn't do their normal routine; he went a different way. They pulled up to a house, and inside was a woman and a little boy who was about the age of two. "Who are these people?" Mary-Ann thought. Her father told her that the little boy was her brother and the woman was his girlfriend. Confusion was her immediate response. It seemed like both her parents were moving on and leaving her behind. The questions of "how and why" filled her mind but, for the first time, she was not bold enough to ask her father anything. In fact, that was her first experience with silence. Mary-Ann found out that on the Saturdays her father had not come to see her, he was in Austin with the woman and the little boy. Heartbroken, she swallowed the pill of not being enough for her father. Maybe that is why he started another family but, nevertheless, she made do with the time she could get with him.

The next couple of Saturdays were quite different and awkward. Mary-Ann never had to compete for her father's attention, but now this little boy was telling her that her father wasn't her father and, every time she called for her daddy, the little boy would yell, "He's not your daddy!" She started to become quiet in nature and it wasn't like her. She didn't know how to express to her father how she felt because, honestly, she didn't even know how she felt. Dealing with the feelings of rejection from both parents was breaking her heart. Each Saturday, she tried to push past it but, the more the little boy spoke, the quieter she got. Things were not the same anymore between her and her father; therefore, she just stayed at home with her mother. Saturdays had now become dry and gloomy. No excitement nor her father. It was just Mary-Ann. As she routinely played with her dolls in her playroom, she paired the Barbies together to make a family—her family. She connected the mother Barbie with the daughter's hand and the male Barbie to the daughter's hand. This was a representation of what Mary-Ann wanted to do for her family. Even though they couldn't be together, she was determined to mend the broken pieces.

She wanted to give "going on a date" with her father another go-around, so she called her father. The two had their routine pick-up stops and on to the house they went. Mary-Ann was prepared for the little boy to silence her again. She brought her journal to write down how she felt just to ignore him. As they came into the home, her father and the woman got into what seemed like a screaming match of who could be the loudest. The scenes of her father and the woman fighting brought back flashbacks of her parents. Mary-Ann started to feel uncomfortable and thought she was the cause of them arguing. As a result, she didn't go back to her father's house for a while. Her father came to get her one Saturday, and the woman and the little boy were gone. Her father became emotional at the departure of his son. During that time, Mary-Ann and her father became closer than ever. Things went back to normal as the two bonded over music, called each other, and continued their Saturday dates. Her heart rejoiced once more to be with the man who made time stop, but it seems the sweetest things never last always.

Her father had met a new woman, and this woman had two girls of her own. One Saturday, as Mary-Ann prepared to go on her date with her father, there was the woman and her two little girls in the car. The woman was sitting in Mary-Ann's seat, the front seat. Her father asked how she was doing and, she replied, "Fine," but her palms became sweaty as she contemplated going back in the house with her mother. It became harder to breathe. It seemed like the air in her lungs were slowly slipping away, and the silence began to fill her again. The young girl, who was once free in her speech and emotion, began to feel like she was being pushed into a cage. She didn't want to be around her father anymore because it was never just the two of them. She called her father occasionally, just to hear his voice. She missed him but he hurt her as he started to spend their day with other people.

She was about nine years old at the time when her father

introduced her to, yet, another woman. Although Mary-Ann hated sharing her time with her father, she allowed it because the women were nice and they talked to her, but this one didn't talk to Mary-Ann much. In fact, when she first met her, she didn't even smile, so Mary-Ann just observed her. This woman stayed around longer than the others. Maybe this was getting serious. With this new relationship, Mary-Ann didn't feel comfortable around her dad anymore. When she would spend the night at her father's house, she'd stay up all night and wouldn't sleep until she got back to her mother's house. This became a routine as she would stay over. She didn't see her father consistently after that because she was never alone with him.

Mary-Ann was 12 years old now, and her relationship with her father was hanging by a thread. She did not speak up about the things that bothered her, yet, she just hoped he could see she was troubled. He called one day and asked if he could pick her up, and Mary-Ann prepared herself. The car ride reminded her of the days with her dad when she was younger but, this time, she was a little quieter. When they got to the house, she saw the woman and she looked like she had put on extra weight, but again, Mary-Ann just observed her. Later that day, her father said something that finally shut the cage and silenced her. He told her that she might be having a little sister or brother. Unable to comprehend her emotions, she swiftly ran away from the man she loved. The walls began to close in on her and the smoke of anxiety began to fill her lungs. Was this her last breath? Her heart shattered. She struggled to pick up the pieces because, every time she tried to make sense of it all, the pain cut a little deeper. She was the only girl her father had but, with the other woman and now the possibility of a baby girl, Mary-Ann knew she was no longer at the center of her father's heart. The arms that once held her tight were squeezing the blood from her heart. "Am I really not enough?" she questioned. She sat outside as she tried to gather her thoughts. She looked at the woman and thought this was all her fault. "You took my daddy away once and now you're taking him away forever," she thought. Mary-Ann called her mother and left her father's house. Months later, the woman gave birth to a baby girl, and Mary-Ann was now mute and numb. The arrows of pain, disappointment and grieve no longer hurt; it was now a part of her growing pains.

When she entered middle school, she become rebellious in nature while crying to her journals and diaries. With the lonesome feeling she received from both her parents, she no longer spoke up about how she felt. She only spoke to her journals, no longer to people. She painted a mask for the world, while every tear she cried exposed the paint. Quickly hiding the rivers of water, she became an actress, acting out in roles of attitudes, eye rolls and dismissiveness. There was a new role in the play of rejection—silence. She did not have to audition for it because she lived it so effortlessly. Her lines were few and the spotlight was now on her as she stood before the crowd in silence.

2.

Silence

The silence was unbearable. Screams from the top of her lungs could only be heard from her journal but felt through her actions. "He didn't love me anymore, nor did Mommy," she pondered. "Why couldn't I see that from the beginning? It was obvious." These were some of the many thoughts that constantly plagued her mind as she sat in class, on the bus ride home, and even while she brushed her teeth before bed. Whenever she spoke, it was as if her mouth opened, but no words were formulated. She struggled to make sense of her new normal. Everything happened extremely fast. Finally, when her words began to connect, they were cut dry and short lived. She only had three phrases in her vocabulary: "I'm fine", "I'm okay", and "everything is okay".

Her math teacher was doing some exercises on the board as Mary-Ann was thinking to herself again. Before she knew it, the teacher had called on her and was waiting on a response. With every eye piercing at Mary-Ann, she nervously responded, "Everything is okay!" Confused by her answer, the teacher moved on to another student. Mary-Ann embarrassingly placed her hands over her face in hopes that it would make her invisible, but it didn't. The truth was she wasn't fine, she wasn't okay, and everything around her was falling apart. The class period had ended, so Mary-Ann promptly grabbed her bag to go to her next period class. Reaching for her bag, she saw another hand. She looked up to make eye contact with the owner—it was her teacher's. Trying to hold the floods, the barrier broke, and tears fell from her eyes. Before the teacher could ask her any questions, she broke loose from her backpack and headed for the restroom. "She'll know," Mary-Ann sniffled. "Stop it. Everything is okay," she reminds herself as she surfed through the crowd of rambunctious 6th graders. Her teacher found her, and Mary-Ann only answered her questions with "everything is okay." Since the next period class was beginning, the teacher didn't press to ask her anymore questions. She handed Mary-Ann her backpack and said the cliché statement, "I'm here whenever you're ready." Mary-Ann politely smiled and nodded in agreement. As she walked away, she clinged to the straps of her backpack while tears began to fill her eyes. "Today's journal entry should be interesting," she quietly whispered to herself.

It was the last day of school and the final bell rung. "On to 7th grade!" Mary-Ann thought as she made her way home. As she entered the house, she dropped her bookbag at the door and headed straight for her room. Laying on her bed, she reflected on how she almost exposed herself to her teacher. "That was a close one," she sighed. She counted the cycles of the ceiling fan until it gave her a headache. "It's summertime," she thought. "What am I going to do? Who am I going to spend it with besides Mommy?" Summer break was normally a time Mary-Ann would look forward to as she got to escape her routine life at home to hang out with her father, but the once familiar man became distant in feeling and touch. With his new life and family, he became unrecognizable. How do you move forward when the heartbreak comes from your father, when the one man you love makes you feel invisible and unimportant? No more dates, no more pick-ups, just alone in her room listening to the music she and her dad once shared. She hoped he'd be listening to the same song too.

Mary-Ann had been talking to a friend of hers that she met when she was in third grade. Ever since the third grade, she always had a crush on Calvin Till. They kept in communication all throughout the summers when school had let out. She enjoyed his conversations, but he was a bit advanced than her. He was two to three years older than her and had already lost his virginity. Their conversations switched from being rated PG to rated R. He began to ask her for things she wasn't ready to do, but he continued to pressure her. Because of the pressure and the crush she had for him, she sent him a picture of her pre-mature body. She was afraid and scared. "He sees me now," she sobbed. "I did not want to do that, but there's nothing I can do now." She felt uncomfortable and regretful but, to have someone to talk to, she was willing to be uneasy. This was the branding of the title "man pleaser." It did not make sense then, but it was soon to be clear as she got older.

As the last song played, the lyrics of Sizzla's "Give Me a Try" were stuck in her head. "This is a sign to call Daddy," she thought as she unplugged her headphones. "Maybe the lady and baby were gone?" Mary-Ann thought, "You know, like the lady and the boy." Mary-Ann convinced herself enough and built the courage to call her dad. It had been painfully long since she had spoken to him, and her heart was beating as if she was going to be speaking to a stranger.

She rehearsed the conversations and how smoothly everything would be.

"Hello Daddy." ...No, I sound silly.

"Hi Daddy." ...No, I sound too desperate.

"DADDY!" ...Definitely not, I don't want him to know I miss him.

She rehearsed until she was confident enough to call. Hearing his voice again for the first time in months made her cold heart flow with blood again. Nervously, she said, "Hi Daddy, what are you doing?" "Nothing, what's up?" he responded. She built the confidence to say what use to easily roll off her tongue, "Daddy, can you pick me up?" His response was different, one she hadn't anticipated in rehearsal, in fact, one she had never heard before. He responded, "Make your mother drop you off." Mary-Ann responded, "Uh...uh...okay?" As she hung up the phone, she questioned her reasoning for calling him to begin with. She felt played and taken for a joke, but she still decided to go see her father. Her mother dropped her off, and she watched the rear lights of her mother's car fade into the unknown. Realizing she had been standing in her father's driveway for five minutes, she shook of the nervousness and marched to his front door. She took a deep breath and whispered, "Here goes nothing." Her voice cracked as she screamed, "Daddy!" She tried to behave as normally as she could, but she was greeted with, "Shh, the girl is sleeping." Mary-Ann's father never punished her or even went as far as to tell her to be quiet. Immediately, she knew her father wasn't the same man. Awkwardness filled the living room as she and her father looked at each other. Mary-Ann desperately tried to pick up where the two had left off, but that boat had since sailed. She did not have his attention anymore. While they would talk, his attention was elsewhere. One ear was in the conversation while his mind was on the baby. He periodically interrupted Mary-Ann as she tried to update her father on her daily adventures as a 12-year-old, but he didn't care anymore, and it showed.

Mary-Ann witnessed for herself the last drops of blood from her heart bleed from her eyes. She went to the bathroom and called her mother to pick her up, then waited outside for her. As she waited, she sat on the front porch and played with the kittens. Her father came to hug her goodbye and she held him a little tighter just to see if the old him would come back. Just as the memories of her and her father began to resurface, it was interrupted by screams of a hungry baby. He let go and she ran to her mother's car. The ride home was silent. Mary-Ann looked outside the window as every image of her and her father began to reflect against the window. As she reached for it, she could hear the laughter of her three-year-old self and that of her father's, but reality kicked in and it was just her imagination. She went home that night to write in her journal with an entry titled "It's over."

"No more laughter. No more smiling. All I hear is a baby crying. I reach for your image, but it's only my imagination. Please, when will this all be over so I can reach my final destination? I fought in a war with you, all in violence, but it seems as though you don't see me because you have a new alliance..."

Her heart was broken. How could this relationship change this drastically? Mary-Ann decided to take breaks in visiting her father, hence she went every six months. As she continued to see her father, she longed for their connection but, every time they spoke, she saw she was only beating a dead horse. He didn't listen to her nor pay attention to the things she would say. He would ask her to repeat herself and she would reply with never mind. Their relationship continued like this for a while, but Mary-Ann continued to push through it. Her baby sister was now turning a year old and Mary-Ann was now 13. The family came together and threw her baby sister a party to celebrate this milestone, and some of her father's friends came as well. Mary-Ann was always excited whenever her family would come around because, growing up, it was just her and her mom, so seeing distance relatives always made her happy. It was time to take a family photo with the birthday girl and everyone was getting adjusted when, suddenly, Mary-Ann felt her father's friend rub himself on her. Mary-Ann, in disbelief, didn't want to take pictures anymore, so she left. Later that night, she went home to tell her mother what happened, and she advised Mary-Ann to tell her father and, with a nervous heart, she did. Mary-Ann called her father the following day.

"Hi Daddy, I gotta tell you something."

"Okay, what is it?"

"Umm....umm...Daddy, your friend came up behind me and rubbed himself on me."

"Mary-Ann, no he didn't!"

"Daddy, yes he did! I'm not lying!"

"Mary-Ann, I'm not going to argue with you."

She dropped the phone and, with tears rolling down her face, she screamed, "Mommy, he thinks I'm lying!" She cried on her mother's lap as she rubbed her back and, from that day, she never trusted her father to tell him anything. Whenever Mary-Ann wanted to speak to her father, he always assumed that she wanted to argue but, really, she was stating how she felt. Did her feelings really mean that little in the world? Her father's unbelief in her was the driving force of her being silent about everything to come because she thought, "If daddy didn't believe me, why would anyone else?"

3.

Abuse

By the age of 13, she was officially considered a teenager. She was still the same girl, you know, quiet and always writing, but her look began to change. It seemed as though, overnight, her structure became that of a mature woman, like the waves crashed against her to form every curve. She was beautiful. Maybe she had always looked this way, but she never took notice until the boys did. She began to receive an overwhelming number of compliments about her shape from both younger and older women. Her family members would say, "Girl I wish I had that shape." They'd tell her father, "I hope you got your shot gun ready." He'd smirk and say, "Yeah, I'm ready." With the compliments no longer coming from her father, but from outsiders, it began to solidify and validate who she was. She enjoyed the attention, but maintaining it was beginning to be a full-time job. Some days, she just wanted to be herself but, in order to be remembered, she just accepted it with a smile. Her audience was no longer focused on her but on what was hers. This made Mary-Ann quickly become uncomfortable in her own skin. "At least no one forgot me," she thought quietly to herself as she walked down the hallways filled with testosterone-inebriated wolves. "Things could be better," she said, "But at least I'm remembered."

Mary-Ann would go over to a family friend's house often, whom she met from church, because they had children around her age. On Saturdays they would go dancing, and Sundays they would be in the church house. One Saturday, Mary-Ann decided to go with them. They dressed her up and she wore some of the older girls' clothes because it complimented her shape. The girls would say,

"Dang girl, look at you!" Mary-Ann looked at herself and it seemed a bit much, but she loved the way the dresses would hug her body. Since her parents didn't talk about their homelands much, Mary-Ann did her own research on the culture. She learned the way they spoke, what they ate, their music, and how they danced. Mary-Ann had been practicing the moves she learned for quite some time and she was ready to show the world what she had mastered. As she entered into the party, people would stare at her but wouldn't say anything. She went to the center of the floor and began to move her waist like that of a cyclone. Whenever the guitar would play, she would draw in her prey. As she continued to master her skill, she would receive many compliments on how she could move uncommonly swiftly, but with control. She didn't go with them very often, but this was the birthing of her love for dancing and how she would attract men. There was freedom when she danced and a form of distraction from her pain, because she understood the power she had in her waist. Being West African and Caribbean, or "exotic" as people would call her, it was almost a requirement that she knew how to dance. It was for the culture. She picked up her dancing shoes occasionally, but, Monday through Friday, she was the most studious of them all.

Fast forward to her last year of middle school: eighth grade. She was 14 years old and began to hide herself more as she developed. It was embarrassing. She was torn between loving her shape because other people told her it was beautiful and hiding because it seemed people forgot about her and only remembered her shape. She questioned why other girls looked like a thin slice of bread and she was the loaf. She clothed herself in things that hid her figure, so no one really knew what she looked like anymore. The attention then transitioned to her swiftness in thinking and how intelligent she was. She was at the top of her class and a certified leader. However, with every great leader, there's always a kryptonite, and she was soon to find hers. She had a new excitement in her eyes. It wasn't an ordinary sparkle either. It was one that makes your adrenaline rush, giving her a feeling like she was on the top of the world. You know? The kind that makes everyone invisible and all your cognitive skills eject from your mind. Are you picking up what I'm putting down yet? Yeah, I'm talking about a boy.

Sigh. It begins.

She had a crush, a love interest, and a new found distraction from her pain. Her mind was filled with happy endings, wedding bells and babies. Wait, wait, wait. I know you're probably wondering, "Dang, does she even know his name?" Don't worry, I got all the details.

His name was Leon Mackintosh. He was the cutest 13-year-old boy she had ever seen. He was sweet and understanding. He had a smile that could light up the whole room, and he always knew how to make her laugh. Her shape was one that caught his eye, but he loved her laugh. Knowing she was easily tickled, he told the corniest jokes just to hear it. Leon lit up her dark world, and she told herself she was going to marry that boy. He was very shy whereas Mary-Ann was more outspoken around him. They were opposites, but they found a balance. She never wanted him to think she needed him, but she loved having him around. His patience was something she admired about him since she was very easily tempered. The one issue about him, though, was he smoked, and Mary-Ann didn't agree with the behavior and gave him an ultimatum: her or the drugs. Conclusively, he chose Mary-Ann.

They spent every day talking to each other. After school, he'd wait with Mary-Ann until her mother came, then he'd dash off into the darkness without being spotted. Mary-Ann wasn't allowed to talk to boys, but she bent the rules for Mr. Mackintosh. After talking for two weeks, Leon popped the question. Well, not that question, but it was close enough. He asked, "Will you be my girlfriend?" Mary-Ann screamed and danced around her room and, after five minutes, she responded, "Yes!" Her journals collected dust as she began to speak to Leon more about the things she faced. Leon was her best friend, and she let her guard down completely with him. The two went on dates to parks, to the movies, to concerts, or just cooked food at his parents' house. Mary-Ann also developed a close relationship with Leon's mother. Mary-Ann and Leon's mother had open conversations about everything ranging from sex, contraceptives, and any other things that were considered taboo to talk about with parents. It was overwhelming at first because, you know, Mary-Ann wasn't used to that type of conversation with a mom, but she loved the honesty and felt close to her. His mother shared that she and Leon's father met at the same age as Leon and Mary-Ann, and she was incredibly happy to see them together. She spoke to Mary-Ann about the two getting married, since she and Leon's father never did, and how amazing it was going to be for her and for Mary-Ann and Leon. Mary-Ann thought, "If she believed it, it will come to pass." She felt a sense of family whenever she was with Leon and his family. After scars were left on her heart from her dad, she never thought she would be able to be loved by anyone, but Leon loved her. He was her safe place, where she could be her true self.

Every Friday, Leon would use his allowance to bring Mary-Ann a bag of Hot Fries and a Twix. Her face was filled with excitement every time he brought it to her because it reminded her of her father. It didn't matter how many times he did, she just loved being thought of. Valentine's Day had rolled around and the couple was reaching their one-year mark. Longevity and consistency was something she had never seen, thus this was a definite sign he was the one. On Valentine's Day, he brought her roses, a teddy bear, and a jumbo card with their picture on it. Her heart melted at the love he had for her. It was something indescribable. The two would attend church together every Sunday with Mary-Ann's mother, and they would talk about the sermons that were given and how excited they were to see each other. This seemed like a match made in heaven.

For their two-year anniversary, he had gotten Mary-Ann an infinity promise ring, roses, and an iPod Touch. The young couple, Leon, 15, and Mary-Ann, 16, both virgins, knew they wanted to be in each other's lives forever, and nothing was going to get in the way of that. The two made a promise to wait until marriage because they were too young for sex, but since they planned to get married anyway, the wait was no longer necessary. Her first experience was not what she expected. She thought everything would be like the movies, but she loved him so it didn't matter. Mary-Ann's love for Leon had grown to a new level. She trusted and leaned on him more. It was as if she was attached to him at the hip. She hadn't experienced this kind of love, therefore she held closely to it. They didn't attend the same high school, and it made things a little strained. Insecurities began to rise within Mary-Ann as she witnessed Leon be extremely friendly with other females. It reminded her of her father, and the shortness of breath started to kick in again. Over the course of the relationship, Mary-Ann didn't realize that she made Leon her only friend, while Leon had a multitude of friends. Communicating with others was hard because she made him her only friend and the only person she spoke overtly to.

Over the course of several months, the relationship became overwhelming and the arguments began to intensify. Mary-Ann began to push Leon away and she guarded herself. She didn't want the familiar feeling of being disposable to resurface, so she began to slowly shut down. Leon was no longer her safe place, or her secret keeper. She could feel her heart being emptied again, but this time it was removed completely. The two decided to go on a break and the sun had set forever. While the couple was on break, Mary-Ann took it as an end and decided to learn new things from someone else. While she was at work, she met a guy who expressed interest in her. She found him to be alright looking, but she wanted to talk to him to see if something was wrong with her, since she did not find pleasure with Leon. The two exchanged numbers and she told him from the jump, "I just want to know if something is wrong with me." He was a preacher's kid, but he was no saint. He was 22 years old and eager to assist Mary-Ann in finding out if something was wrong with her. It was different. He was not sweet, kind, or Leon, but it was like the movies. She sucked it up and continued to learn because this was strictly business. The distance became too overwhelming for Leon and he decided the two should work things out. While Mary-Ann was at work, Leon came over to surprise her after work. He picked up her iPod and decided to go through it. Finding text messages between Mary-Ann and this preacher's kid, he left her, and her soul left with him too.

Mary-Ann had never experienced this kind of pain or heartache. Leon's mother came to visit Mary-Ann, and she sat in her car to express to her how she felt. "Yeah babe, you messed up. The best thing to do is give him some time and space," said Leon's mother. She cried to his mother and pleaded, "I'm trying and I'm sorry. I know I messed up, but we weren't together." His mother responded, "We were good to you. Why would you do that?" Mary-Ann didn't know how to tell Leon's mother that he didn't know how to satisfy her, so she just sat in silence. His mother hugged her and told her she loved her. Mary-Ann told her she loved her too, and left to go back inside her mother's house. The weight of death hung low all over her body as she witnessed Leon be with other girls. From the neck down, she was numb. She knew he was no longer loving her but someone else and it killed her. Not having her family anymore was really the thing that sent Mary-Ann into a deep depression. She didn't know how to talk to her mother about this pain because she would normally speak to Leon's mother but, since everything happened, she knew she couldn't speak to her because Leon was her son, and she needed to be there for him. She figured the only way to eradicate this pain was to physical remove herself. Two suicide attempts. Nothing worked. She laid on the floor and hoped that maybe if she didn't move, her body would shut down. Her mother found her on the ground and screamed her name. She was alive, she just wished she wasn't. Her step-father had given her mouth-to-mouth resuscitation, and she laid limp. The fire department and the ambulance came. As she heard the voices of firemen call out her name, she only wished her heart would stop beating so she wouldn't hear them anymore. They blew something in her nose and she jumped up from her stillness coughing. They put her on a stretcher and rolled her outside. She looked up into the starry night and wished she was in the sky with them. The EMT asked for everyone to give them privacy as he talked to her in the ambulance. He told her, "Mary-Ann, nothing is wrong with you, what is really going on?" She confessed that she had messed things up with Leon and how she felt like her life was over. He reminded her that we all make mistakes that we are not proud of, but we move on from them. He hugged her goodbye and reassured her that everything will be alright, and this was going to pass. She later confessed to her mother as well, and a shadow of relieve passed by, but the black cloud was still there. Screams of frustration she shouted to God, "Why am I still here? What do you want from me?" Depression became her lifestyle as she just lived day to day. She blamed herself for everything. Losing the only person who ever loved her truly and her family killed her because she knew she would never have a love like that again. She started to think that if anyone were to love her again, she should be grateful because she deserved nothing.

Life just didn't seem worth it anymore. Mary-Ann attempted at getting Leon back. He still attended church with her, but they didn't talk much. When her mother would drop her off by his house, she would beg him to take her back, but he didn't budge. She asked if she could see his family, and he agreed. She went inside and walked shamefully to his parents' room to say hello, and they reassured her that they didn't hate her or think anything bad about her but, no matter how many times they tried to convince her, she still didn't believe them. After that, Leon came in and out Mary-Ann's life like a revolving door. Emotionally, it was abusive and draining because he knew she was apologetic, but he just continued to play her like a fiddle until he got all he wanted. A couple of months go by, and Leon moved on with someone else. It was best that she did too. Life was never the same for Mary-Ann, and she never thought peace would be her song again. She was now 17 years old and he was 16. It had been a year since she had seen Leon. He messaged her, and her heart lit up.

"Hey, how are you?" Leon asked.

"I'm fine, how are you?" She replied.

"I'm great, I don't have any classes for the day. What are you doing?" He inquired.

"I just finished my class for the day, why?" asked Mary-Ann.

"I'm coming to get you. See you in a few!" He sang.

Mary-Ann was confused, but also excited. She never thought she would ever see him again and, now that she had the opportunity, she was ready to redeem herself. Leon came to get her, and it was a little awkward. He had her favorite song playing in the car, and she awkwardly smiled and said, "You remembered." Leon was more outgoing, and Mary-Ann was shy. He took her back to his parents' house but, this time, he took her through the back door. Mary-Ann was a little alarmed, especially since she had never been hidden before. His parents had finally gotten married. It was Leon's mother's dream, and Mary-Ann wanted to tell them congratulations, but she didn't have that opportunity because they didn't even know she was there. The two sat on the couch in the garage, and Leon begins to go for a kiss. Mary-Ann quickly moved and asked why he was doing that. He asked if she wanted him to stop but, because she had not seen him in a while and she was still in love with him, she let him have his way. He showed her everything he had learned since the two had been apart and, after it was over, he told Mary-Ann, "Alright, well, I gotta go." Mary-Ann responded, "Go where? I thought you were finished for the day." He responded, "Yeah, but I gotta go." The two got in the car, and he drove her back to her school. During the drive, they had a mild conversation.

"So… what are you doing later?" Mary-Ann asked.

"I have a cooking date with this girl I'm interested in," Leon replied.

Silence overcame the car.

"You have a what? What the heck did you pick me up for then, if you have a date, you freaking idiot?" Mary-Ann exclaimed.

"I just wanted to hit it one last time since I won't be able to," Leon declared.

A floozy, harlot, good for one thing, a good time, and every adjective for a sex worker you can think of, is what Mary-Ann felt. She wanted to cry, but there were no more tears left. She just sat in silence. "Maybe this is what I get," Mary-Ann thought. "Kind of my pay back." They arrived at her school and he says, "Have a good day." She got out and slammed the door. A pain that cut too deep couldn't be described. She had never felt this disgusting in her life.

Over the course of time, she stuck with the label of being "just a good time" and a "man pleaser" as she felt unworthy of real love. She felt that whoever she ended up with was a gift from God, and she should be grateful that anyone who would want her. Her pain was one she couldn't easily express through words, hence why she expressed herself through sex, even when she didn't want to, which was ninety-five percent of the time. With every guy she met, she held them to the standard of Leon, but they never compared. She stopped looking for a relationship because it never moved passed the talking stage. They always had one thing in mind, and she was never strong enough to say how she truly felt. She just let them have it.

For spring break of 2017, Mary-Ann had decided she wanted to go to Saint Lucia, where her father is from, to visit her last set of living grandparents. Her father told her to send all of her information to her uncle's wife, since she would be the one booking the flight. She was uncontrollably excited to finally go visit her extended family since she always wanted to. Her uncle's wife asked for information that Mary-Ann wasn't sure she was supposed to send her, so she asked her parents to make sure. She called them and they advised her to send her all that she was asking for. Her uncle's wife sent, in a mass group chat, when everyone should clear their schedules and get ready for their vacation. However, as the time got near for the trip, her uncle's wife lied and said Mary-Ann did not send the information, so she did not get to go. Her spring break plans were cancelled, and she wondered when she would ever see her grandparents.

Since her original spring break plans were cancelled, she needed to come up with something else to do. Throughout the years, she kept in contact with Calvin Till, her third-grade friend. He seemed to always come back around every year, and this time she was glad that he did. She was alone and, to have a familiar face around, she felt comforted. She invited him over one day since her mother was away at work, and this was the first time the two were seeing each other since elementary school. He always talked about the things he wanted to do to her and, when he saw her, that's exactly what he had in mind. She brought him to her room where she wanted to watch whatever was on TV but, as soon as he got in her room, he began to pull down her shorts. She kept telling him to stop but, the more she said stop, the more aggressive he got in pulling down her shorts. Finally, he succeeded and entered in. She was still and just laid there as he finished up his last couple of strokes. She figured, since they were talking then, whatever he wanted, he was obligated to take, even if she screamed no. The next time she had sex with him, she did not feel anything. In fact, she told him, "I forgot we were having sex." He got a little offended, but it highlighted just how numb she had become.

In the summer of 2017, a year after things officially ended with Leon, Mary-Ann thought she found the one when she had encountered a guy by the name of Sammi, but she was soon to find out he would only play with the strings of her heart for seven months. The first night she met him, she was with her friend, London, and they had just attended the Class of 2017 Graduation ceremony. London wanted to see the guy she was talking to, who was friends with Sammi, and Mary-Ann, just being bored on a summer night, stated encouragingly, "Let's go!" London bought beer and the two headed to go meet the boys. The music was blasting in London's car, and Mary-Ann began to dance and sing along to the music. They arrived at the boy's place, and Mary-Ann thought the house they were parked in front of was their house. She danced and kept watch for the door to hear when it opened, and to stop so they wouldn't see her. They came from the house across the street and said, "Oh, that's how you feel?" Mary-Ann jumped and blurted "Omg no. This is embarrassing...Hi, my name is Mary-Ann." London thought she was trying to be a showoff but, really, Mary-Ann didn't know the boys lived across the street and would see her. She apologized and London just replied, "Let's just go in."

The girls walked in the house and the guys began to inquire about her. This made London jealous, as she felt no one was talking to her and Mary-Ann was taking all the shine. They asked if the girls wanted to smoke, and Mary-Ann, being inexperienced, looked to London. London, answering for both, said, "Yeah, we will." Mary-Ann turned to London nervously and panicked. "I don't know what I'm doing!" London replied, "I got you babes. I'll be with you, don't be nervous. You don't want to show them that." Mary-Ann took her first hit and she felt nothing, so she stopped, went back in the house. The boys decided to go upstairs, and the girls followed. Mary-Ann sat on the floor on her phone and London was on the bed with Sammi's friend. Sammi began to talk to Mary-Ann, and they realized they had gone to high school together. Mary-Ann told Sammi she never talked to him because he looked like a "player." Sammi smiled, "Nah, I'm really chill. I'm not like that." They continued to talk for a while before things took an unexpected turn. It was now five in the morning the next day, and everyone was awakened by an incoming call. It was London's mother. The girls got up and got dressed. They kissed the boy's goodbye and drove home quickly. Mary-Ann had never done anything extra daring or spontaneous, so she became intrigued with this guy. The two continued to engage with one another, and Sammi taught her how to smoke. Mary-Ann had turned into someone she'd never imagine herself to be. When the two weren't having sex, Mary-Ann couldn't talk to him or express herself. To tell the truth, it became harder for her to even let him in. It seemed the more he got it, the less they talked, and it bothered her because he didn't know her and she wanted him to. She questioned him about why he hadn't asked her to be his girlfriend and he confessed, "I don't deserve you. You're too sweet for me and I'd only hurt you." She was confused. After giving herself away, how could he say that? Whenever they would try to get to know each other, it was like pulling teeth, and he would ask her why she did not talk much. Truth was, she didn't want to open up just for someone to leave again. She didn't want to burden anyone with her pain because she knew they wouldn't understand or care. He didn't know how to cut things off with her, so he lied and stated, "I think I may have caught something while smoking with someone." Mary-Ann was furious. "How could you do this?" she responded. "How could you put me in danger like that?" He never said anything about it, except that he was sorry and that she deserved better. It began to remind her of what Leon did to her, as he came back to her only for sex. To drown the memories, she began to self-medicate with alcohol whenever she was with her friends, and drugs when it was available.

In that same summer, her little sister was celebrating her birthday, and her father invited her to go to Galveston with him and his family. Mary-Ann decided, "Why not take a free trip?" While there, she tried to talk to her father about how he made her feel in the past. Every time she spoke, he shut her down by saying, "I'm not going to argue with you because that's all you want to do." She didn't want to argue, she just wanted him to listen to her because no one ever did. She did everything he and his family wanted to do, so, one night, she wanted a chance alone with her dad while everyone was sleeping. She asked him if he wanted anything from the store, hoping he would accompany her, but instead he responded, "Get me some pork skins. I'll stay up and wait for you." Disappointed in his response, she walked from the hotel to the store alone. The hotel was on 46th street and the store was on 118th street, so you can imagine the walk she had. It was dark, but the city was lit with restaurants and clubs that were filled with people. She finally reached the store, and got everything she wanted and, on her way back, she got a call from Leon.

"Hello?" She answered.

"Hey, are you at home?" Leon asked.

"No, I'm in Galveston. What do you want?" She questioned.

"I wanted to stop by and see how you were doing," he stated. "What are you doing in Galveston?"

The two stayed on the phone until she got back to the hotel, which took an hour and a half. She told Leon how he made her feel when the two last met up, and he apologized and said he never meant to make her feel that way. She was pleased to hear him acknowledge his wrongdoing and sympathize with her feelings. Mary-Ann asked Leon to say her full name because he made a promise, when they were younger, that he wouldn't say it until he proposed to her. He did not say it, which meant he still had feelings for her and, maybe one day, he would want to reconcile things. A spark of hope filled her heart. "Maybe he and I can work things out," she thought. She always kept that in the back of her mind over the years and, without recognizing it, everything she did was in preparation for him to choose her again. Zealously, she waited for him. When she finally made it back to the hotel, she was vastly excited to talk to her dad, but she found him asleep and her heart broke once more. "Wow, he couldn't even wait for me. Anything could have happened to me," she sighed. The following day, they packed their bags and headed back home, and Mary-Ann got ready for the upcoming school year.

Senior year came around and she was 18 years old, officially an adult. Life had gone on, but her heart hadn't beat since she was 16. She didn't think about the happy endings, marriage, babies, or anything anymore. She didn't feel worthy of that lifestyle. Actually, marriage wasn't even a thing to be considered anymore. She figured some day she might get married but, if she did not, it was not a big deal. Life goes on.

Mary-Ann had ended things with Sammi, and she was ready to prove to him that he wasn't the only one who could move on. After school one day with London, she decided to create an account on an online dating app just for jokes, not really thinking anything of it. She met a man name Martin Edmond. He was a 20-year-old, handsome, caramel-skinned man with beautiful teeth. He was tall in stature, 6'3" to be exact, with big broad shoulders. He was from Mississippi, a country boy with southern hospitality as his persuasion. "I definitely hit the jackpot with this one," she proclaimed. "He's tall and fine? I think yes!" He was something like a mountain that she wanted to climb, but Mary-Ann didn't realize he was not just a mountain figuratively, but Martin was indeed her mountain— a roadblock from peace. As she began to converse with him, she quickly realized she wasn't his type of girl. His persona was one that was hood rich, while Mary-Ann was suburbia's finest. She recognized the difference but, if he were still talking to her, then maybe it could work. He disguised himself as an angel of light but, really, he was the one that fell with Lucifer. During the weekdays, they called him assertive, but on the weekends, his name was abusive.

4.

Denial

After talking to each other through the app for some time, Martin asked for her number to hear her voice for the first time. The first night the two spoke on the phone, Mary-Ann felt like a school girl. It had been a month since she had talked to a guy, and she enjoyed not feeling alone anymore. Mary-Ann always had someone to talk to. She moved on quickly, so she never had to deal with the pain or the void she felt in her heart. Martin started off as something different. He was a little rough around the edges, but she didn't mind the roughness. Speechless at how attentive and sweet he was, she wanted more from this southern man. Martin stated he wanted to take her to her favorite restaurant. She blushed and replied, "I'll check my schedule and see where I can fit you in." Mary-Ann had nothing to do, but he didn't need to know that. "I'll make him wait for a response," she said. She loved the sense of control she had in the beginning because she was tired of someone telling her how to feel or what to think. Mary-Ann called Martin and agreed to go on the date, then she called London to give her the 411. Mary-Ann screams as soon as London picks up the phone. Startled, London screams as well. "What is it?" London inquired in a slight panic. "He asked me on a date!" exclaimed Mary-Ann. "What should I wear? How should I do my hair and makeup?" "Girl I'm coming over!" London shouted exhilaratingly.

The girls stayed up trying on clothes to see what would complement Mary-Ann the most. "I like the black and white one," London cheered. "It makes you look THICK." Mary-Ann practiced how she was going to walk in the restaurant. "Look strong, but not too strong," London said. "Men like women who easily submit."

Mary-Ann reflected, what did they know about relationships anyway? They were only eighteen and seniors in high school. "Loosen up, girl. You look scared." The girls laughed. "I'm trying to do what you told me to do," Mary-Ann giggled. "Girl, I'll just walk how I walk, and you just tell me what to wear."

The day of the date had come, and Mary-Ann looked beautiful. Her fro was slicked back into a low ponytail and her eyebrows were arched perfectly. She had that sparkle again. Her smile was back, and her glow could be witnessed from miles away. Mary-Ann and London pulled up to the restaurant to come up with a game plan in case Martin was a lunatic. London was going to sit at a distant table behind the two to watch. If anything got crazy, London was to pop off on Martin from behind, and the girls would dip. "Girl, you gotta be careful. These dudes trifling," said London. Mary-Ann just smiled. She knew that to be true all too well.

Martin had arrived to the restaurant early so the two could have beautiful seating. He texted her and said, "I'm here." Mary-Ann screamed, "Girl, he's here!" London replied, "Okay babes. You're going to kill it, and know I got your back! Knock 'em dead." She spoke to Mary-Ann as if she was going for an audition, but I guess it kind of was if you think about it. Mary-Ann adjusted herself and replied to Martin's text, "Coming!" As she walked to her table, she whispered silently to herself, "Shoulders back and booty up." She walked with purpose, one leg in front of the other. She was balanced. The walk to the table took ages, it felt like, but she didn't mind the runway. As she walked, she repeated to herself "look strong, but not too strong" until it was engraved in her mind. Martin's eyes pierced every portion of her as he gazed in amazement. His beautiful smile pushed through his rich lips, and he stood up as a Hyperion when he went to greet her. With Mary-Ann being only 5'5", she caught every whiff of his cologne. "O-m-g," she thought to herself, "he smells deliciously good." She held on to him for what felt like 20 seconds. Realizing the length of the hug, she let him go. "Wow, you're stunning," he said in his southern accent. He sounded like an angel but, little did she know, he was the angel of death coming to kill everything she had ever worked for. Mary-Ann smiled and said thank you. He replied, "Get whatever you want. Don't worry about the cost." This was different, he was different. He was not like Leon or any guy she talked to, and Mary-Ann was overly optimistic.

Nonetheless, Mary-Ann was nervous. She hadn't been on a date before, nor really held a conversation with a guy. She never had the opportunity to because it was always just sex. He made small talk and asked her about her day. She responded but, while she was talking, she noticed he kept staring at her. She paused and asked, "Why are you staring at me?" Martin replied, "I'm listening to you. Yeen ain't never had nobody listen to you before?" Truth was, no, she hadn't, and it was freaking her out that he was. Martin saw her weak points, which he'd used to his advantage in the future to keep her enslaved in insecurity and bondage. She was nervous because he was starting to recognize her weaknesses. She rushed to eat and Martin halted her saying, "Hold on, Miss Lady. We gotta bless the food first, ma'am. You like to eat, I see." Mary-Ann was extremely embarrassed. She normally would pray for her food, but she forgot. His initiative intrigued her. They laughed and Martin began to pray. "Lord, is this him?" she prayed to herself as she watched him from across the table. "Is this my husband?" After dinner, he walked her to her car and hugged her for a lifetime. It was cold, but his hugs were her heater. He said, in his southern accent, "I hope I see you again, Miss Lady." She blushed and replied, "It'll be my pleasure, sir." She got in her car and watched him happy dance back to his. She rested her head on the head rest and smiled to herself. London came running to the car and the girls screamed. London said, "Dang girl. Was the food that good, or was he that fine?" "Both," Mary-Ann smiled. As she was about to fill London in on the rest of the date, there was a knock at her window. It was Martin. She opened the door, and he jumped and squeaked, "Who is that?" Mary-Ann laughed and introduced him to London. He introduced himself, in kind, as a gentleman. He later asked London, "You mine if I steal my lady from you real quick?" London replied, "Do your thing. She looks like she wants you anyway." Mary-Ann slapped London's arm, and Martin pulled her close to him, grabbed her face, and kissed her and said, "Goodnight, Beautiful. I'll call you when I get home." Filled with butterflies, she replied, "Okay, sir. Drive safe." London looked at Mary-Ann and Mary-Ann smiled, "Girl, that might be the one."

After the dinner, things moved faster than Mary-Ann anticipated, and Martin became more impatient as the time went. He wanted her to come over, but she really wanted the two to get to know one another first. She didn't want to repeat the cycle of giving herself away and then watch the person leave. She wanted to be treated like Leon used to treat her. He got to know her awhile before they had sex. She compared every guy she met to Leon because he was the only real thing she had. Martin was leaving for the Army soon. He whined about how he was going to miss her, and how he planned an early Valentine's Day celebration just for the two of them, since he was leaving in March and his mother wasn't going to be home. Mary-Ann didn't really want to do anything, or go to his house but, with his persuasion and persistence, she fell through. Mary-Ann told London that she was going to spend the night with him, and she wanted him to pick her up from London's house because she didn't want him having her address. Mary-Ann told her mother that she was spending the weekend with London so, after school, she drove to London's house.

"Are you scared?" London asked nervously.

"Yeah kinda, because I don't know him," Mary-Ann expressed.

"I'll give you my pocketknife and, if he do anything suspect, jab 'em where the sun don't shine," London advised.

Mary-Ann's phone lights up with a message from Martin.

"He's here. I gotta go," Mary-Ann mumbled.

"Share your location with me, and call me at every chance you get," London begged. "Have fun and text me if you feel uncomfortable."

"I will, don't worry. Love you," Mary-Ann replied.

"Love you too," London said.

The girls hug each other and Mary-Ann leaves.

Mary-Ann walked outside to Martin's car. He got out and grabbed her duffel bag to put it in the trunk. They got into the car and Martin asked, "How you doing, Beautiful?" She responded, "I'm fine, and you?" He responded, "I just got better." Traffic was heavy. It was 4:30 p.m. and she looked out the window thinking, "Mary-Ann, what are you doing? You met this man off the internet, girl, and he could hurt you." She remembered the knife she had, thus a sense of comfort hugged her for a bit. He asked her what she was thinking about, and she answered nothing but, really, she was thinking how to escape him if he was a serial killer. She looked in his car and he had some gadget on the floor connected to his system. She asked him what it was, and he said it was a police detector, which alerted him whenever police were nearby. At that point, she was certain this man was bat crazy, but she was already in the car, so let's see how this goes. The conversation was very dry. She asked the general questions she only knew to ask a guy, which was about his sex life. He told her about all his daring stories, and how he was almost close to getting caught in some of them. She didn't know what other questions to ask because she never had the opportunity to really talk to a guy. They stopped at Walmart, and she called London to update her.

"Thank God you're alive," London exclaimed. "I've been watching your location. What you doing at Walmart?"

"Girl, I have no idea, but he didn't let me go in with him," Mary-Ann explained.

"Well, how is everything?" London inquired.

"It's going great, but I'm curious to see how this night ends," Mary-Ann confessed. "Girl, I see him coming. Love you, gotta go."

Martin came back and hid some things in the back. He giggled, "Don't look, it's a surprise." She smiled and said, "Okay, I'm not looking." The two were getting closer to his apartment. He stopped at a convenient store to get orange juice and bottles of alcohol. She texted London to let her know what was going on. Shortly after, Martin came back, and they headed to his apartment. Before he took everything upstairs, he told her to wait and he would come back to get her. She waited for 20 minutes and thought, "Lord, please don't let this boy come and kill me now. I'm too young. Please." Martin came back and said, "Come on, Pretty Lady. Everything is ready for you." He led her up to his room and opened the door. Rose peddles covered the floor, and roses, a card and a bear sat on the bed. She turned and smiled at him and blurted, "Aww! Thank you." The two ate Chick-Fil-A and watched Vampire Diaries. He poured them some shots and she took each one to the head. The rest of the night was a blur. She couldn't remember anything; all she could remember was them eating, and then everything went black. Waking up in the middle of the night, he asked her to be his girlfriend. She cried and said, "Yes, but please don't hurt me. I've been through too much." He held her close and reassured her that he would not hurt her or do anything to disrespect her. All he wanted was for her to be his for eternity. On the ride home the next morning, she began to feel a feeling of regret and shame. As he was driving, he reached for her hand and clasped his and hers together, gently planting a kiss on her hand. Thinking to herself, she groaned, "Time for the countdown." She knew the time stamp on this adventure was soon to expire because she had given it up. He dropped her off and she told London everything.

He left for the Army and was stationed in Georgia. He wrote her letters and, on the envelope, he gave Mary-Ann his last name. She screamed with excitement, and she felt ready to spend a lifetime with him. Over the course of him being away, he began to exhibit behaviors that were not pleasing. He became controlling and manipulative, accusing Mary-Ann of cheating and having other people. She was confused and hurt. "Why would he say that?" she asked herself. She figured that him being at boot camp, far away from home, was having a negative effect on his emotional well-being. Consequently, she became accepting of the behavior. He began to talk down to her, call her weak, and compare her to his mother. The girl, whose shoulders were once back, became like a low-hanging fruit. She had been talked down to for months, and it became a norm to her. She answered to everything he called her as if it were her name. London would do weekly check-ins to see how the couple was doing, and Mary-Ann couldn't tell her that he was actually not who she said he was, so she kept his behavior a secret, and fed her lies about a perfect relationship.

Throughout the many accusations and constant degradation, he'd apologize and say that he doesn't know what's going on with him. He thanked her for staying with him through his storms, and promised he was going to better himself for her. He admitted to her that he had demons and she, having somewhat of a prayer life, prayed that God would deliver him. She never prayed for herself, always him, in hopes that God would see her praying and He would bless her in return for it someday.

The season came for Martin to graduate from boot camp, and for Mary-Ann to graduate from high school. His graduation was a week before Mary-Ann's and she wanted to support him. The school administration threatened Mary-Ann saying that if she left, she wouldn't graduate, but she took the risk for him. She needed to get to him to show him just how much she loved him. She gathered the money she had saved for college, and put it towards her transportation and stay in Georgia.

When she first got to Georgia, she called him with much excitement because that was the first time she had heard his voice in months. When she finally met him to pick him up, she ran to give him a hug, but he pushed her off saying soldiers weren't allowed to show affection in their uniforms. Embarrassed, she apologized and got in the car. He kissed her and said, "Sorry baby, it's a regulation." She thought it was stupid, but she went with it. The two ate and went back to her hotel to catch up on the time that was lost. Mary-Ann was on her cycle, and this was just going to mess everything up. She told Martin and he challenged, "A period ain't stop nothing but a sentence." Awkwardly she submitted and responded, "Okay." After an eventful evening, she had to drop him off due to his 7 p.m. curfew, which didn't leave them with much time to spend with each other since they couldn't talk on the phone either. The next day was his graduation. She got up early to dress herself up as the most beautiful girl he had ever seen. She met his stepfather and FaceTime with his mother during the ceremony, because she was not able to make it for his graduation due to work. His parents were sweet to her and she finally felt like she belonged. Now that she had taken the big step of meeting his family, she excused the mere thought of Martin's treatment and behavior towards her. She stayed with him for three days, and his behavior seemed to have changed. It seemed he just needed to release some steam. "All it took was patience and prayer," she sighed. During the stay in Georgia, she became his personal chauffeur, and drove him everywhere he wanted to go. She didn't mind driving him around, but she wanted to venture through the city with Martin. He made every excuse as to why he couldn't, and that they should just stay in the hotel and catch up. She felt like he was hiding her, possibly even ashamed of her. She denied and ignored every gut feeling just to please him because, if he was pleased, her mind could be at ease.

5.

The Truth

After Martin's graduation, he thanked her for being there to support him. He told her, "I'm going to marry you, Baby Girl. You're everything to me." Mary-Ann smiled to herself, but there were signals going off throughout her body telling her to leave him. She put the signals on do not disturb and continued with her trip. It was her last night with him, and the two had one last go around before she dropped him off. He hugged her tightly and whined, "I don't want you to leave. I'm gonna miss you. You're my star." She replied, "I know, but I have to." As they got in the car, he directed her to take him to a different location, one she hadn't dropped him off at before. Some of the other soldiers were there. She got out to hug and kiss him goodbye when his comrade's mother gasped, "So, you're the beautiful girl he keeps talking about. What a pleasure to finally meet you." Mary-Ann smiled, "Yes ma'am, I am. I hope he's been telling you good things." The two exchanged hugs, and they talked for a while before it was time to go. Mary-Ann got in her car and went back to the hotel to enjoy the rest of her evening in peace and quiet.

Back at home, senior year was ending, and it was time for prom and graduation. Mary-Ann went to prom with her friends. Martin had warned her to be a "good girl" and to not do anything stupid or he would handle her. Mary-Ann thought the aggression was cute in the beginning, but she never knew it was a testimony to his character. Martin didn't attend her graduation, and he didn't even tell her congratulations. It bothered her but, to keep face, she told everyone it was because he was on assigned duty. His absence made her feel stupid and senseless. Days before her graduation,

Martin called her because he was allowed to use his phone. He fussed at her, talked down to her, and belittled her. She sat on the phone and took every ounce of it like a child. He later apologized for his behavior and, with tears in her eyes, she forgave him. "It's just the pressure of being away from family," she said to herself. "He doesn't mean it."

"Class of 2018, you may now turn your tassel," ordered the Student Council President. Mary-Ann had just graduated, and her family rushed to greet her. Her mom, aunties, uncles, cousins, sisters and, most importantly, her father were all there. "I'm so proud of you, my girl," her father grinned. "You never cease to amaze me." Hearing those words from her father was medicine to her pain. "Thank you, Daddy!" She gushed. Her father and mother had a graduation party for her, and she invited Martin's mother. It was the first time the two had met physically since speaking to one another on the phone. Mary-Ann introduced Martin's mother to her parents and spoke with her the whole night. She got to know her a little better as she asked her about her background and what she did for a living. Martin was pleased that his mother liked Mary-Ann because he never introduced anyone to his mother, which made Mary-Ann feel special. His mother confessed, "Martin must really like you because he hasn't introduced me to anyone. I was beginning to think something was wrong with him." Martin asked for photos of the two of them, and Mary-Ann was beginning to feel a sense of closeness with his mother. This new relationship reminded her of the relationship she had with Leon's mother, and she craved for that kind of relationship with the mothers she would come across. "This was perfect," Mary-Ann thought to herself. She sent photos to Martin and he responded back, "My queens." Mary-Ann felt things were getting better, but they were soon becoming worse.

Mary-Ann had been working at a pizza joint since her junior year of high school. She continued to work there during the summer, until she went off to college. One day during her shift, she received a text from Martin. Her heart lit up and she responded back quickly.

"Hey baby, how are you?" Martin questioned. "Hey babe. I'm fine, and you?" Mary-Ann replied. "I'm fine… I gotta ask you something," Martin warned. "How much do you love me? Like, really love me?" Confused she replied, "To the moon and back. You know this!" Mary-Ann got a strange feeling from the text. "Why is he asking me all these questions?" she asked herself. "Would you still love me if I was a daddy?" Martin probed. "Somebody said I'm their baby's father, and I just wanted to let you know."

The world stopped, and her heart froze. Mary-Ann asked her manager if she could step outside to call Martin. She called, but he didn't pick up. He told her he had to talk to his mother first. Mary-Ann, enraged, questioned, "What does your freaking mother have to do with this? I'm your girlfriend for crying out loud." He told her he didn't want to talk to her and didn't respond back. Left confused in her car, her eyes took the color of a blood moon. She FaceTime her friend, Mia, and screamed, "He has a freaking baby!!" Mia, confused by what Mary-Ann was saying, asked her to slow down. Mary-Ann's heart was racing. Her sentences were incomplete, the world was rapidly spinning, and she was losing control. She couldn't explain her feelings to Mia, all she did was scream. She went back into the store and told her manager she had to go. No one asked her any questions or said anything.

Martin sent photos of the child. He was a beautiful baby, and he kind of looked like Martin too. She just hoped he wasn't Martin's baby. Later that night, Martin called and apologized to Mary-Ann.

"You don't deserve this," Martin indicated. "You deserve better. Just leave me. I don't deserve you."

"You dang right, you freaking idiot. How could you do this to me?" Mary-Ann scorned. "I'm sorry," Martin sobbed. Mary-Ann was fuming with anger and had no rebuttal for his apology. "So, what you gone do? Leave me?" Martin challenged. "Just let me know because I can't do this."

Out of fear of being alone, she told him she'd stay with him. Meanwhile, the signals came back, but she could not afford to be alone again. She became okay with the possibility of a baby mama. She asked him if he would get tested to see if he was the father, but he reassured her that he and his mother already took care of that. He said his mother was hoping the baby was his because, after having him, she hadn't been able to have any children, and she felt the child was from God. Mary-Ann thought to herself, "What kind of Looney Tunes circus act is this? I pray that baby ain't his." Mary-Ann never heard of the baby drama anymore. Who knows if he was or was not the father? It just sort of got swept under the rug like everything else. The arguments continued, but Mary-Ann felt that he had the potential of being a good man. He just wasn't there yet, and she was willing to stay around until he became that man. She had invested time into him, so she was determined to see the return of the man she wanted him to be.

Shortly after his graduation, he was stationed in South Carolina for three months and, after his time was up, Martin was planning to come and see Mary-Ann for 10 day, before being stationed in Asia. She was excited to see him and to be with him. He was crazy, but consistent, so she didn't mind. However, she had been stuck in the house dealing with Martin and his shenanigans all day. She just wanted to get out and have some fun, so she invited her cousin to go with her to an Independence Day event later that day. Before getting ready for the evening, Mary-Ann was at her father's place playing with her little sister, who was now six years old, when she received a direct message from a girl in the country that Martin was soon to be stationed in.

"Hi. I don't know you, but your boyfriend is cheating on you. I didn't know he had a girlfriend. I am so sorry." Mary-Ann sighed and responded, "Thank you for letting me know."

She sent Mary-Ann screenshots of messages and pictures she received; it was all from Martin. She could feel the breath in her lungs slip away as the last straw in her straw house started to cave in. She sent everything to him. "What is this?" She questioned. "Are you serious right now? You freaking moron! I'm done with you." Mary-Ann's heart was drained. She was tired of fighting. Enough was enough. His mother had visited him in South Carolina and, because she was around, he declined every call. Mary-Ann called him at least a hundred times and, finally, threatened to tell his mother. He responded to her and pleaded, "No, please! I'll call and explain everything later." Later finally came and the performance began. He cried and confessed how sorry he was, and how he made a bet with some friends that he was able to "pull a girl." He asked if she could forgive him. Indeed, he was sorry and pathetic, but the fight was too much, and Mary-Ann didn't want to forgive him. She just wanted to be free from the chaos and from all the heartache he had caused her in only five months. She wanted peace, but where do you find it? Ultimately, she forgave him again and continued to get ready for her evening. When she finished, he asked her to send a picture to him and his mother. He posted it on his Instagram and captioned it saying, "This is my girl, my everything, my star. All you other "hoes" need to back back." He deleted the post three weeks after that.

Martin was back in Texas, and Mary-Ann was excited to see him. It seemed like every time she saw him, she never remembered his lies, disrespectfulness, or abusive nature. The first night, Mary-Ann got all dressed up for him, only for him to stand her up. "It's okay," she said. "He's probably busy with his family."

The third day, Mary-Ann wanted to surprise him. She wore this beautiful rose-colored dress and left her house at 12 p.m. to head to his apartment in Dallas. She texted him all morning and afternoon, but he didn't respond. She stopped by a Chick-Fil-A and waited for him in her car for two hours in the Texas summer heat. By the time he finally responded, it was 2 p.m. She never told him that she had been waiting for two hours because she was going to look dumb. He told her he wanted to take her to a hotel and have her all to himself, so it made up for the two-hour wait. She dropped her car off at his apartment and got in his. He didn't even notice her outfit. He rubbed her thigh and finally complimented her, "You look good. I'm about to get you out of that, though." She smirked and rolled her eyes. "Yeah, whatever," she thought. They pulled up to a Motel 6 and she felt extremely disrespected. "Did this dude really just bring me here with all the money he has?" She never focused on his money but, come on, a Motel 6? She didn't say anything. She just smiled, but she was definitely disgusted. They got in the room and he announced, "Get comfort and be ready when I get back." She inquired, "Where you going?" He had to go to Auto Zone up the street, and he said he would be no longer than an hour. That hour turned into four hours later, and the Auto Zone was only down the street. She called him and texted him, but he didn't respond. Alone in the room, she drank more than half of the Fireball he had on the counter and whatever else was there. She began to play music and dance in the room by herself. She was sad and lonely, but the alcohol comforted her. Finally, Martin returns her numerous phone calls.

"Aye baby, my car ran out of gas down the road," Martin revealed. "Can you come get me?"

"What that gotta do with me?" Mary-Ann slurs. "Oops, hey babe."

"Girl, are you drunk?" Martin interrogated. "Did you drink my liquor?"

"Maybe a little bit, but you left me!" Mary-Ann confessed. "I was bored. What was I supposed to do by myself?"

"Bro, what? Nah, since you want to drink my stuff, get up and come get me so I can go get some gas," Martin insisted. I'll deal with you later."

"No, I'm intoxicated," Mary-Ann emphasized. "I am not driving, boy, you can walk."

"Girl, I'll see you when you get here," Martin argued as he hung up the phone.

Mary-Ann got dressed and drove to get Martin. She cried as she drove and cracked a window, hoping the cold air would sober her up. She pulled up to Martin's car and he gave her an ear full.

"Who told you to drink my stuff?" Martin shouted. "Are you going to buy me some more?

"No," Mary-Ann stated firmly...

"Exactly, so why you touching stuff that's not yours?" Martin drilled.

After he filled a gasoline can, he ordered Mary-Ann to take him to a convenient store so he could buy some more liquor. She told him that she didn't want to because she was drunk, and it was dark, but he said he was teaching her a lesson to not do it again next time. They pulled up to a shabby store and he went in. She rested her head on the steering wheel and wished he would just hurry up.

She didn't care that he was mad. She was having fun because he was stressing her out, so if drinking his drinks got him mad, oh well. He came back and told her that drinking was not who she was or what she does. That lifestyle was for him, not her. He told her he loved her, and only made her drive because he didn't want her to drink again. They got to his car, filled his tank, and headed back to the motel. He saw all she had drank and chuckled, "Yeah, I'd be drunk, too, if I drank all that." They laughed and he kissed her and told her to rest while he went to get some food that'll help her sober up. She rested but woke up still alone. It was now 2 a.m. and Martin was still out in the streets. He called and asked if she was hungry. She hadn't eaten anything, so of course she was. He promised he'd grab her something on the way back to the motel and it shouldn't take him long. She trusted his word and waited for him, but he didn't come back until 4 a.m. He looked high or tipsy, but she couldn't tell because, with either, he looked the same. Mary-Ann was on her cycle again, but it didn't stop him from grabbing her. He fell asleep afterwards, and she was up alone eating the hamburger and fries he got her. As the sun took its place in the sky, they checked out of the motel and headed home.

On the fifth day, the two went out to bowl. This was the first public outing they had done together since he normally wanted to hang out at his apartment. She felt like his trophy, like he was excited to have her on his arm. He was being sweet and kind to her. She hadn't seen this side of him since they first started the relationship, and she loved it. As the day became night, it was time to go home. Martin's car was giving him trouble, so she drove the couple around yet again. Mary-Ann wanted to drop Martin off back at his place and go home, but he had other plans for the night. As she got to his apartment, he told her to pop her trunk. Confused, she obliged. He called her name and told her to come to the back. She was still on her cycle and was not in the mood to do anything. She stood her ground for the first time and refused his sexual advances. She just wanted the two of them to hang out and catch up without any sex involved for once. Her lack of consent infuriated him. His tone changed and he told her he was going to leave. She pleaded with him to stay and that he was ruining their moment. She wanted to just enjoy the rest of their night together before she had to go. Her soft-spoken voice enraged his demons, and it seemed like, every frustration Martin had, he released it on Mary-Ann's neck as he forced her head into her driver-seat window. Tears rolled down her face in disbelief at the monster that was before her. She saw fire in his eyes and rage fill his body. She begged him, "Why are you doing this to me? You're hurting me." As he loosened his grip off her neck, he objected, "I do it all the time during sex, so why you crying now?" If he would've kept pressing harder, she would've lost conscience, but he loosened his grip and vanished into the darkness. He always joked about wanting to kill her, but that night was a glimpse of what he had in mind all along. Mary-Ann eagerly drove away from his apartment and went home. At a stop light, she didn't realize it wasn't her turn to go, but she went anyway. Three pairs of headlights shined on her and she screamed. Seeing her life flash before her, she thanked God for His protection, because it was as if an arm was the only thing blocking all three cars from smashing her into pieces. The ride home was silent as she contemplated her relationship with Martin. This was the beginning of the custody battle for her body. Many times before, when she never wanted sex, she never spoke out about it. With this being the first time she ever said no, she was afraid of what would happen if she did not feel like living up to the title "man pleaser." That same day, Mary lost custody over her body and her sense of control. From that moment forward, if anyone wanted anything, she did not fight or resist. She laid vulnerable and did what she did best: please.

The next day, Mary-Ann went to visit Mia and told her what Martin did. Mia advised her to tell Martin how he made her feel, and Mary-Ann knew she needed to, but she just couldn't. She told Mia she would, knowing she never will. Martin later texted her. He never apologized. He just texted her and said he wanted to take her on a picnic date since he knew she always wanted to go on one. She went to see him, and he drove to Walmart to buy the food and the blanket. His smooth talk had her back in his arms again, and they laid on the blanket as the day turned to night. He wanted her, but she was on her cycle still. It seemed like every time he wanted her, she was on her period. Maybe it was a sign or protection from what was to come. Who knows? But whatever it was, she always disregarded it. She gave him what he desperately wanted out of fear of him hurting her again. Her signals went off again. This time, she knew she needed to leave, but how?

It was time for Martin to depart for Asia, and Mary-Ann took him to dinner. He cried the entire night, "I don't want to leave you." Mary-Ann felt a peace in her heart. She wasn't sure why, but she did. She told him everything would be fine, and he would be great. Later that night, he wanted her again and, this time, he drove to an abandon location in the dark and took what he wanted. At this point, it was just something she gave away because, if she didn't, he would abuse her again. She wanted to see him off the following morning, but it didn't work out that way. He left for Asia for a year, and she had finally come to terms with the truth of his behavior. The truth was, he didn't love her. She was just something he used to get pleasure from but, with college coming up, she had bigger fish to fry. "Finally, some peace and quiet," she thought as she prepared for her new life— college.

6.

Broken

Mary-Ann was packing up the life she once knew and was preparing for the one she had not much prepared for. It was time to leave for college and utilize all the tools she learned. The only thing she heard about going away to college was the freedom, a new life, a career and sex. Other than that, she had no idea what to expect. She hadn't given much thought to what she wanted to do with her life. She thought she wanted to be a doctor, but that was the role everyone had given her, and she just took it. "Did I learn anything?" She often questioned herself. "Am I even ready for this?" A new life was beginning, and she was going to be on her own, not that being alone changed anything, because she was used to that. It was the decision-making part that scared her. Everyone had always told her how to feel, what to think, what to be, and how to act. Now, having the power to decide for herself made her nervous.

The remainder of her summer was sweet. She didn't hear from Martin because he couldn't use his phone much, which worked in her favor. He'd text her occasionally, and she'd looked at the notifications and roll her eyes. She loved the power she now had. He was under her control and demand. He spoke to her with respect and allowed her to say her piece. She wanted to get rid of him, but she didn't know how. While she prepared for college, Martin expressed his fears of her moving on and finding someone else. Her main concern was finding peace, not other people, but it was nice to know he was worried about her finding better. They both knew she deserved it.

Move-in day was here, and Mary-Ann was nervous but excited.

Many emotions rushed in at once. When her mom had left, she looked around the empty room. Her little life was packed up in boxes, and she didn't know which to unpack, so she just laid on her new twin size bed and hoped they would unpack themselves. She didn't have a roommate; therefore she had the big room to herself. Not knowing what to bring for accessories, her walls remained cream colored and bare. When she graduated from high school, she also received her associate's degree, leaving her with two years of college to finish. The university had a freshman orientation for incoming students. She was a junior by credits but, since it was her first year there, she had to go to the events for freshmen students. Interacting with people was hard. She was self-conscious about everything: her hair, her clothes, and even the way she spoke. Speaking to people made her nervous, and it was hard to develop friendships. To gain some friends, she got her feet wet in the pre-semester events the organizations had on campus. She attended a lake party that a Greek organization was having, and she made sure to step out. "He'll know exactly what he's missing," she smirked to herself as she did her makeup and hair. She looked supremely beautiful. Her yellow two-piece swimsuit complimented her cocoa skin. She never felt confident in wearing a two-piece swimsuit but, just to annoy Martin and boost her confidence, she did. The stares and the compliments made her feel above life. Some asked for her number, but she politely responded, "I have a boyfriend, sorry." "Why am I even being loyal to this loser?" she mumbled to herself as she sat on the bench, going through her and Martin's photos. He was crazy, but consistent. There was a guy who was passing out shots of vodka and, being that she wasn't really enjoying herself, she told him to pour her some. He held her head back and poured it in her mouth. She lifted her head and laughed as she thanked him. She had an Instax Mini camera, and the guy took a photo of her with it, which he kept to remember her. She found it awkward but didn't think much about it. She had gone there with some girls she met, and one of the girls was talking to a friend of the guy who poured her the vodka. The girl wanted to go smoke, but Mary-Ann didn't want to. However, since she was the designated driver, she took the girls. The girls went upstairs to the guy's apartment, and Mary-Ann texted Martin as an excuse not to go in. She texted him to call her ASAP, but he told her he'd call her in a little. The one time she needed him, he wasn't where there so, out of pressure, she went upstairs. There were four guys in the apartment, but Mary-Ann made sure to label herself as unavailable. They started smoking, and they passed the blunt to her, but she rejected. They passed it around again and, out of fear of being the only one who wasn't high, she hit it. She was now six blunts in when Martin called. Her heart dropped because she knew he would be upset to see her high and, out of all the ways he could've called her, he decided to FaceTime her. "Perfect. Just great. He's about to chew me out," she groaned as she answered the call.

"Hey baby, sorry I couldn't answer the phone. I was trying to figure out transportation," Martin explained.

Trying to act normal, Mary-Ann steadily, but hurriedly replied, "Hey babe, you're fine. I just wanted to see how you were doing. I love you."

"I love you too, Baby Girl, but where's your face?" Martin questioned. "And, what's all that noise?"

Mary-Ann smiles with cherry colored eyes. "Hey baby...."

"Bruh, you high, and it's dudes over there? Alright. Live ya life."

Martin promptly hangs up.

Mary-Ann tried to text him and explain herself, but he wasn't trying to hear it. Yeah, he had a reason to be mad, but... well, there are no buts. He was right. She went back outside to the group and stated she had to go, so the girls left. She sprayed herself down before walking in the resident hall and walked with her head down. Who was this new girl? Martin called and allowed her a chance to explain herself. He knew she didn't cheat, but he was upset that she smoked. He told her not to hang out with the girl anymore, and she didn't. Great way to start the semester, huh? Well, let's see how everything unfolds.

It was the first day of the semester, and she was stunning. She put forth an effort to look her best but, by day three, she was tired of dressing up. Martin would ask for pictures of her and she sent them to him. "My wife is beautiful," he said. "Like wow bro. Look at you." She blushed and thanked him. Things were going great, and he was on his best behavior. She had no complaints. Towards the third week of the semester, things started to get a little rocky, and Mary-Ann was sick of the repetition. In late September, two weeks before her October birthday, she met this guy named Kameron after her dance try out for the Caribbean Student Association organization on her campus. He came there meeting someone else but, unbeknownst to him, the girl had a boyfriend. When he got there, he stared Mary-Ann down, and she and a friend asked him what he was staring at. He smirked and reassured, "My fault y'all, wasn't trying to stare that hard." Everyone sat and talked for a while then everyone left one by one. It was now Mary-Ann and Kameron. The two ended up talking and getting to know each other up until 2 a.m. in one of the university's buildings. She asked him if he had a relationship with God and if he had a church home, since she had recently found one on campus. He said no, and she invited him to hers. It was pretty late, and she had an 8 a.m., so she went to her room. He tried to walk her to her door, and she declared, "You're good where you at, homeboy. See you later." They had exchanged information, although he knew she had a boyfriend.

He'd always asked when she was going to leave him, but she just laughed and replied, "Boy, shut up." Martin was still getting on her nerves, but Kameron was just a good friend to have around. Kameron had asked to hang out with her one night and, at the time, she thought nothing of it. They were just friends. What could happen? She had her laptop propped up with Netflix, along with some snacks and drinks ready, for them to just watch a movie. He came over to her room, and the two sat on her bed and watched scary movies. She laid down and Kameron followed suit. As she was watching the movie, she felt him forcibly trying to get in her shorts. Alarmed, she asked, "What are you doing?" Realizing they were not on the same page, he replied, "Oh, my fault. I thought you wanted that." Mary-Ann looking at him and shouted, "No, I was watching the movie. Please, just get out and leave." He left, and she just sat on her bed. "What have I gotten myself into?" she pondered. Kameron was the first and only guy she had good conversations with. Besides the dumb thing he did, he was an alright dude, hence why she forgave him.

One night, she went out to dinner with one of her girlfriends she hadn't seen since middle school. The two talked about their old memories from school, and Mary-Ann posted a video on social media of her and her friend at the table. Martin immediately responded, "Who the hell else is at the table?" She replied "What do you mean? It's just us." He concluded "Yeah, alright Baby Girl. Play me like I'm stupid. It's cool. All that food on the table, you expect me to believe it's just y'all? Do ya thang. I ain't even mad." Mary-Ann, hiding the frustration on her face, decided to end dinner early with her friend. On the way back home, she called him.

"What's up?" Martin laughed.

"What is your freaking problem? Mary-Ann shouted. "I'm out with my friend, and you acting stupid!"

"If yeen did nothing, why you worried? Martin floats dismissively. "It's cool, Baby Girl. I'm chilling. Live ya life."

Martin abruptly hangs up in Mary-Ann's face.

The sky was filled with much rage as it released a sound of thunder, and so did Mary-Ann. It was a sound of annoyance, frustration, and a plea for her freedom. "God, what is going on?" she asked. "Why doesn't he get that I love him, yet he just treats me like dirt?" She didn't love him. In fact, she had no idea what love was. She only had an imagination of what it was and, when he called and apologized, she forgave him once again. Two days before her birthday, enough was truly enough. She called his mother and requested, "What do I do? He doesn't listen to me, only you." His mother responded, "Mary-Ann, there is nothing holding you two together. Leave." When Mary-Ann first met his mother, she told Mary-Ann, "Although he is my son, I would never advice you to stay." Mary-Ann didn't understand what she meant at the time, but she now realized that she had given her a warning.

It was her birthday. She was 19 and ready to celebrate stress-free. Martin told her happy birthday, and she thanked him, but she was over him. Mary-Ann finally built up the strength to break up with him. He called and beg her not to leave him. Like a broken record, he promised he was going to better himself for her, but she was sick of it. It felt good to finally let go of the dead weight but, unfortunately, she was soon to find out she couldn't get rid of him that easily. Mary-Ann never could stay away from men, it seemed. She never allowed herself to heal. She just kept it pushing. Kameron wanted to take Mary-Ann to breakfast and a movie to make up for his behavior. Kameron was tall with a deep hue and a beautiful smile to complement. He stood over Mary-Ann like a tower, and his hugs restored her pain. After breakfast, they went to

the movies and, of course, she still did not know what to say to guys; therefore, she asked the general question about his sex life. He told her his story and returned the question. Maybe he wanted to know what kind of girl she was, so she told him. Later that night, they came back to her room and she gave him what he wanted. She did not feel bad about it this time because, despite what he did to her in the beginning, she still
thought of him as a great person.

Kameron finally took Mary-Ann up on her offer to come to church with her and, after the service, he immediately ran up to some girl. Mary-Ann knew in her gut that he had sex with her before, but she was waiting for him to tell her. He ran after Mary-Ann to her room, and she asked, "Who was that?" He responded, "My best friend." She was not buying all that nonsense. She declared, "You've had sex with her before, haven't you?" Perplexed, he responded, "Huh? How you know that?" She rolled her eyes and boasted, "Because I do, but that doesn't matter because you're here now with me." The two had spent majority of their time together when classes were over, and they had gotten much acquainted.

The Caribbean Student Association was going to have a Wet Fete and Mary-Ann was excited to go because, finally, she got to do something related to her father's culture. Wet Fete is a big Caribbean party with music, drinks, and food, and you wear little to nothing or things you do not mind getting wet and dirty by paint and water that will be thrown at you. Mary-Ann was ready to throw her waistline at anyone that came her way, and it seemed as if every guy at the party was lined up to dance with her. She was drinking and enjoying herself. She was free. She did not care who saw her. One guy, in particular, wouldn't leave her alone and snatched her away from every guy she danced with, so she danced with him for the rest of the night. Towards the end of the party, he chased her down to get her number, but she wasn't interested in him. It was just a dance that didn't mean anything. She went back home and told Kameron what she did, not that she needed to, but she did out of respect for him since they were always with each other. Nevertheless, he wasn't her boyfriend. After service one day, they came back to the room, and Mary-Ann had just had an emotional breakthrough in church. Kameron stayed with her to make sure she was good. He asked her if she was okay and she just nodded her head. He went on to say, "I have to tell you something." At this point nothing could surprise her. She had seen the worst of the worst and she was ready for whatever.

"I really like you, and I've been having feelings for you for quite some time now," Kameron confessed. "You're very sweet, smart, and you got a good head on your shoulders. I want you to be my girlfriend."

"Oh my gosh!" Mary-Ann gasped. "How long have you been holding onto this, and why haven't you said anything?"

"I was nervous and didn't know if you felt the same way," Kameron said nervously.

"Of course, I feel the same way!" Mary-Ann exclaimed.

The two hugged and celebrated over a taco date. As they drove there, he held her hand and looked her in her eyes. This was an upgrade from everyone she had talked to. She was excited that she was finally chosen. After the date, Kameron started spending the night over Mary-Ann's place, and she loved waking up to him in the morning. She was building somewhat of a relationship with God, and she asked him if he wanted to join her in her relationship and he responded, "I already have a relationship with him so..." Embarrassed that she asked him, she just replied, "Oh, okay. Well, never mind." At the time, she was majoring in biology and it was not her niche. She did not understand any of it, and she was about to receive a "D" in her biology lab. She went to talk to an advisor about taking the class again next semester, so she would not receive a "D" on her transcript. She got everything fixed, but she felt like a failure. She came back to the room and met Kameron, who was waiting for her. He knew she felt stressed about the whole situation, hence why he stayed longer to comfort her. She cried to him about her fears of being a failure, and he reassured her and told her about his experiences with classes. She did not say anything else. He just rocked her in his arms as she cried about her fears of life. He, being present during her meltdown, made her feel closer to him. She had never cried in front of a guy about something that bothered her before, she felt a sense a safety with him, and an expectation that maybe this might be the one.

It was now Kameron's birthday, and she wanted to show him just how much she appreciated him. She got him a card, his favorite candy, and she had planned an eventful evening for him. She spent the night with him at his place the night before so he could wake up with her next to him. The two had been having unprotected sex since they met each other because she was on birth control, but she wanted to make sure she was healthy. Mary-Ann set up an appointment to get tested for an STD. She had gotten tested once before, but she had not since Martin and, since she and Kameron couldn't keep their hands off each other, it was best that she did. Two weeks before Kameron's birthday, at her appointment, the doctor gave the instructions. "If we don't call you back, you're great, but if we do, something's wrong." With no worries in the world, Mary-Ann did everything she was instructed to do for the test. On the day of Kameron's birthday, later that day, they called back. She saw the caller ID, but she didn't believe they would find anything because she didn't have symptoms or wasn't the kind of girl who didn't take care of herself or hygiene. Her doctor came on the phone and delivered the news that she tested positive for an

STD— herpes. Devastated she dropped her phone and, in the distance, all you could hear was her doctor saying, "Hello?" Mary-Ann looked at Kameron and screamed, "What did you do? What did you do to me?" Kameron, in shock, knelt down and whispered, "I'm sorry." She pulled away from him as she sobbed on the cold floor of her dorm. He held her hand as she screamed in disbelief. The two rocked on her floor in silence. She wanted to be alone. She couldn't even look at herself anymore. "Who will love me? Will I ever get married now? What if people can tell when they see me?" These were the many thoughts that went through her mind. She began to think of exit routes from life, feeling she couldn't live with this scar. This one was too big to live with. Wrestling with the demons in her mind, she cried out, "Jesus, I know I don't talk to you, but I heard you heal diseases. Can you take this away?" She sat in silence, knowing this was only a problem that God could solve. She deemed herself unworthy for the healing because she didn't talk to Him much, but it was worth a shot.

Kameron got tested and his results were negative. "But how? He was the only one," she cried to herself. Her doctor called again and asked her, "What about Martin?" Devastated she screamed, "How could he do this to me!" She later found out that Martin had been cheating on her throughout their entire relationship. Mary-Ann still had him on Snapchat, and she watched his story where he posted him and a girl eating dinner while she kissed on him, and pictures of her in his car. The girl had two different shirts on in the snaps while Martin had on the same shirt, and she knew he slept with her. This explained why he stood her up when he was back home, why he left her alone in the motel, and why he did not spend that much time with her— he was with someone else. To describe the feeling as pain would not have done it any justice. She was sick and disgusted with herself at how she let all this happen under her nose. She began to think, "This is my pay back for what I did to Leon." Every bad thing that happened to her, she associated it with what she did when she was 16. She never forgave herself for it. Guilt was her comfort and shame were her clothes. She was broken.

7.

Healing

She blocked Martin on everything after learning about his infidelity. When Mary-Ann told Kameron that it wasn't him but her ex-boyfriend, Martin, who gave her the STD, Kameron apologized for her even having to deal with the situation, and he said that he'd be praying for her. She did not even know how to pray for herself. She had a Bible, but she did not know how to read it, understand it, or even have confidence in it. This disease made her feel like a black sheep, like she had a label on her head, and everyone could see her shame. Kameron still came over just to comfort Mary-Ann. He still wanted to be with her, but Mary-Ann wanted to be alone because she did not know how to deal with this new sentence life issued to her. She felt that she was unclean and unworthy of any form of love. She called her doctor's office again to double check if they had the right patient. They did, and it was Mary-Ann. The nurse reassured her, "It's going to be okay. It's not like you're walking around with a label on your head that says you have herpes. You know 85% of Americans live with this and still have normal lives? You just can't have a vaginal delivery like every other mother." Mary-Ann was sick of people telling her what she could and could not do. She told herself she didn't want to live a normal live. She wanted to live a whole life, and that she WAS going to have a vaginal delivery.

She was a very shy girl and quiet about the issues that she experienced, but this was too heavy to hold, she felt maybe this is something she should tell her leaders at her church. She did not talk to them much, so she was putting herself out there with this one by telling them her business. She was scared. She did not want them to judge her or look at her as someone who was wild or dirty because that was not her. She was in what she thought was a committed relationship, but he cheated on her, and she was left to live with the pain and scars. She swallowed her pride and went to her leader to tell him what happened. Her heartbeat like one who had just finished a marathon as she confessed, "I have herpes." When the words herpes left her lips, tears fell from her eyes, and the new reality of her life finally sunk in. She decided it was best to abstain from sex during this time to clear her mind because she had been doing it since she was 16 years old. She made a promise to God, herself, and the pastors to abstain from sex until marriage. It all sounded easy, but the fight was just getting started, and the end was nowhere in sight.

Mary-Ann relayed the message back to Kameron, and he was cool with it at first. She told Kameron, "I'm not having sex again." He responded, "That's cool. I can wait." Realizing he did not quite understand what she meant by again, she declared, "No, like I'm not having sex again until I'm married." Silence entered the room and he responded, "Nah, I can't make that commitment." She was filled with rage and disappointment as she responded, "What do you mean?" He said, "I don't even know if I want to marry you, like I don't know." To hear that the guy you are interested in doesn't feel the same about you is heartbreaking and embarrassing. Feelings of only being a pleasure for men began to resurface in her mind. "Will I ever be worthy for marriage or love?" Was it too much to ask of someone to finally see value in her, for once, aside from just the sexual pleasures she can give? She thought the two were moving towards a relationship but, really, when Kameron asked Mary-Ann to be his girlfriend, he was not asking her in that moment. Rather, it was something they were "working" towards. Why buy the cow when you can get the milk for free, right? He asked, "What do you want to do?" She wanted him to stay, but she also did not want the feelings of not being enough for anyone. She responded, "I just want to be alone and figure this out with no distractions." He agreed with her, and he only texted her every other week to see how she was doing.

It was now Christmas break, and her first semester of college was one for the books. It can be said for certain; it was one she had not expected. She went back home to figure things out and clear her mind of the situation. The more she did not think about the STD, the more she forgot about it. While home, her cousins had invited her to a comedy club and, since the semester was stressful, she decided she needed the stress reliever. She went to the show around 10 p.m. and was enjoying herself, until the comedian made a joke about people who had herpes. Ignominy was her shawl as the room became cold and dark. It never bothers you until it's you. With a nervous smile, she continued to laugh with the crowd, so no one saw that she was the one he was talking about. The show ended at 12 a.m., but the girls didn't want the night to end early, so they went to a hookah lounge. Mary-Ann had not been to one before and she was up for the new experience. As she entered the lounge, the DJ was playing all the jams from Afrobeats, Reggae, Dancehall, to Rockaway. This was heaven for Mary-Ann, as she released her stress and depression through her dance. She did not remember anything when she danced. It was her emancipation from pain. This was her hiding place as she hid from her shame and guilt. She danced and hoped no one could see the tears that filled her eyes in the smoke filed room.

She inhaled the apple mint flavored hookah and exhaled the pain and distress. Through the smoke, she saw a man who had much power in his waist. He controlled his every move and was very smooth with each step. He was Congolese, so she expected nothing short of the best. She had never seen a man like him, and she wanted just one dance with him. She grew up listening to Congolese music and wanted to show him everything she knew. His dance partner was lazy in her steps and it annoyed Mary-Ann. "I wish I could snatch him away from her," she thought. Sometimes, you really have to be careful what you wish for, but let's see if she got her wish. The club was closing, and she was leaving when she heard, "Where's the after-party?" She looked and it was The Waist King. She smirked, "I don't know. You tell me." He jumped up from his couch with his friend and chased down Mary-Ann. He said, "Excuse me, Beautiful. What's your name?" As she continued to walk with her back to him, she yelled, "Chelsea." He finally got her at her car and asked, "You running away from me, Beautiful?" "Nah, you're too slow. Keep up," she replied. The two flirted back and forth until she confessed her real name, and how she wanted to snatch him from his lazy partner. Mary-Ann let him know that she needed a dance partner for an upcoming performance with CSA and, since he could dance, she wanted him to be her partner. He was 27 and she was 19. He wanted to take her to breakfast at IHOP to get to know more about her, but she declined his offer. They exchanged their social media contacts because she did not want to give him her number. Finally, she arrived home that morning at 6 a.m.

A couple of hours later, The Waist King wanted to see Mary-Ann again, and she agreed to meet him. She asked her cousin to go with her, so she wasn't alone with him, since it had only been hours that she met him. She wore an all-black jumpsuit that hugged her perfectly with her waist length box braids covering her back. She was excited to dance with The Waist King and show him how she could make him fall in love with just one dance. They met at a Caribbean club and he order drinks. They automatically moved in sync with one another and she thought to herself, "This is better than sex. This is a man who finally knows how to deal with a girl like me." She danced the night away with him until 2 a.m. She said her goodbyes and went home. After their weekend of dancing, The Waist King asked Mary-Ann for her number because he did not want to message her on social media anymore. She gave him her number and the persuasion began. Meanwhile, Mary-Ann still had Kameron on the side talking to her occasionally. Her plate was starting to get full and something was going to have to give. Out of fear of being alone, she created a system where she would talk to two people at the same time in case one left. It was a defense mechanism to not be caught off guard again. It gave her power over her emotions. Kameron wanted to come see Mary-Ann while they were on break and take her on a date. She was excited because this would be their second official date, and they did not go out much when they were together, so this was new for her. He picked her up and got out the car to greet her. He hugged her tight, kissed her forehead, and said, "Hey, Beautiful." She had not seen this side of him before and she loved it. He was on his best behavior, but what did he want? When they got to the movie theater, they bought the tickets and came back to the car to take some pictures together. She was happy, but she was skeptical because every time she took a photo with a guy, the relationship always ended. After the movie, they grabbed a bite to eat and he drove her back home, but the reality was soon to kick in that he did not want to wait for her. She asked him, "Why did you take me out if you don't want me? You won't wait for me, what do you want from me?" As he cleared his throat and reached for her hand, "I just missed you and I wanted to see you." She demanded, "Let me see your phone." He hesitated and asked why. Mary-Ann already told him about The Waist King, she advised, "You have a free card to be honest. I won't hold it against you." He finally confessed to talking to a girl, and it seemed this cycle was never ending. She just kept hitting dead-ends. Mary-Ann asked to see his phone, and she read the messages between him and the girl.

"Hey Daddy," The girl flirted. "Can't wait for you to come over."

"Just get ready for all the things ima do to you," Kameron responded.

    Heartbroken she threw the phone back at him and he dropped his head. Her tears trenched her shirt as she asked, "Why are you doing this to me? You don't want me, but you play with my mind and confuse me just to get what you want. Why?" He responded, "I'm sorry." She questioned, "What would you tell me if I was your sister? Would you tell me to leave you alone?" Kameron replied, "Yeah. I wouldn't want my sister to be with anyone like me." She asked, "Why are you doing this to me?" She got out the car and insisted she did not want to see him again, but she did a week later at 4 a.m. After that, she finally decided to leave him alone and just focus on herself.

The Waist King wanted to know Mary-Ann more; yet, she

wanted nothing to do with him. She told him if he's looking for a relationship, he isn't going to get one but, somehow, she ended up entangled with this man for two months. He was into making vanity mirrors, and he wanted to teach her how to make one. She took the bait and was snared. They worked on the mirrors for hours and, towards the end of the night, she got to know more about him. They sat in the garage as he opened up to her about his past, his engagement he had to call off, and his walk with God. The whole time she was talking to him, her heart was beating fast because he was a replica of everything she had ever wanted in a man, and the one thing that could potentially ruin it was her STD. They later transitioned to her car because it was cold outside. As they warmed up in her car, she told him, as fear filled her heart, "I have an STD, but I believe that God can completely heal me of it." He looked at her and smiled, saying, "Of course He will, and I don't look at you differently." She let out a big sigh, "Wow. That went better than I expected," she thought. Since getting the STD, her main concern was how her dating life was going to be and if she would ever find "the one." She began to think, maybe she did. They prayed together before she left, and she felt such a relief with him. The two started seeing each other almost every day and talked on the phone all day. Mary-Ann did not realize that the man she once told she did not want to be with, was now someone she couldn't even go a day without. She never had a conversation with a guy who did not want anything from her and, because of it, she was hooked. She told him about her no sex rule, and he clarified, "Oh, I don't even want to touch you unless you are my wife." Her insides were jumping because, finally, there was a man before her who did not want sex. He just wanted to talk, but it all seemed like a taboo. Was this too good to be true?

    He introduced her to his parents and family, which was fast, and it made her a bit uncomfortable. His parents loved her, which wasn't a surprise, but what was his agenda? He would make many future plans about her 21st birthday and their marriage, which also made Marry-Ann uncomfortable. Why did he seem to be in a rush? She loved the enthusiasm, but it all seemed forced and immediate.

For their dates, the two went out to hookah lounges more and, the first night he picked her up, she wore a black bodycon dress that highlighted everything she had to offer. She always wore fitted outfits for men to see her assets. She felt her personality and who she was were not enough to get her through the door of love. Therefore, she used her external possessions to deflect from her internal insecurities. He got out and opened the car door for her. "Wow, you're so beautiful and you smell good," He said. As they were on their way to the lounge, a breeze of melancholy pressed up against her. As they drove through Dallas, flashbacks of Martin began to flood her mind. The Waist King noticed and asked, "What's wrong, Beautiful?" She responded, "My ex lives over here and I hadn't been here in a while. It's a little hard for me to drive through the area." He told her not to worry and he held her little close as they walked into the lounge together. She became intoxicated as he continued to pour drinks. Life was a blur, but she felt normal as she continued to suppress her emotions and live in denial of her reality.

    New Years was coming up, and she wanted to be in a church but, due to her home church not having a watch night service, she wanted to go to The Waist King's. She stopped by her dad's place first and then went to be with The Waist King at his church. Everything was mostly in Lingala, but she didn't mind not understanding. She just wanted to be with him. Hours later, they went out to another hookah lounge to celebrate the 2019 New Year, and the DJ played everything Mary-Ann wanted to hear. The Waist King watched her from a distance as she moved vivaciously. She danced with the smoke and sang with the alcohol. Life hurt, but she felt good in pain. Her cousins had joined her to celebrate New Year, and they brought their own drinks. Her cousin poured her a cup with more vodka than juice to make her get drunk faster, and Mary-Ann felt every sip of it as she went up to random women to dance with them and do the basic drunk girl things. One woman she went up to was drinking Hennessy, which Mary-Ann had never had. She took a sip and a small voice asked her what she was doing, but she just turned it down so she could continue to turn up.

Mary-Ann spent the majority of her Christmas Break with him, and the rule that they had started to get tested. The two would discuss marriage and the excitement to come when the wait was finally over. Though they did not fully immerse into the pool of sexual lust, they dipped their toes in it every once in a while. "Is this what a godly relationship is supposed to look like?" she thought. When it was time to go back to campus, she had asked him to help her move everything back to her dorm, and this would be the first time that he would ever see her room. Afterwards, because he was not able to see her as much, he started coming over to her dorm and spending the night frequently throughout the school week. The more time she spent with The Waist King outside the club scene, the more she realized she did not really like him. He was not her type at all. He was maybe an inch or two taller than her and bald with a goatee. He was not the kind of man she would normally go after, but she was blinded by his waist. He considered himself to be a worship leader and, when he heard her voice, he suggested, "You should come with me to a revival night I'm hosting with a friend of mine at his church. I want you to sing with me." No one had ever heard her voice. She hid it because she had convinced herself that she could not sing and, when he mentioned something about it, she was embarrassed. He always told Mary-Ann, "I see you leading women and hosting women's conferences." She would always smile and say, "Yeah, no, not me." As the time for him to go to his revival quickly approached, she started hanging out with some ladies from her church. They would host prayer meetings together and pray for hours. It seemed, the more she went to these prayer meetings with these ladies, the more she grew spiritually. He had finally left, and Mary-Ann decided to tell him, "I don't think you should talk to me for the three days you'll be gone. I don't want to be a distraction to you as you deliver the word." He fought her back and forth on the issue, but she stood her ground and emphasized, "I'll talk to you on Sunday when you come back." While he was gone, Mary-Ann went to a meeting with the ladies, and that meeting was a pivotal moment in her walk with God. She could not explain what happened, but something was different, and she did not feel the same. When Sunday finally came, The Waist

King called, but something was different. She couldn't even speak to him. It was like she was speaking to a stranger. He noticed her change and asked her what happened, but she did not have an answer for him. He told her that something told him "she's gone." When he said that, she questioned herself. "Who could have told this man this? Was he watching me?" she thought. She finally told him that she could not talk to him anymore and needed to focus on herself. As she was ending things with him, someone wanted to begin things with her. She finally recognized the cycle, and it seemed like, every time she wanted to better herself, a man would be sent her way to distract her, but enough was enough.

This was the first time she didn't speak to The Waist King, and she began to feel bad for wanting to do something for herself for once. It was like she was only created to be a pleaser of men and to not please, felt unnatural. As she was in class, she struggled with convincing herself that she made the correct decision. Ultimately, she left her class early to go to the chapel that was on her campus. She prayed for an hour and felt a wave of relief rush against her, but it was soon to dry up as she walked out and saw The Waist King looking directly at her soul from the inside of his car. Fear handicapped her as she wondered how he found her on a campus he did not even attend. Why did he feel comfortable coming up to her campus when she was not speaking to him? There were students on campus, but she felt alone and unsafe. He spotted her in the midst of her security, and it felt like there was no safe place to run to now. She walked up to his car and asked, "What are you doing here? I told you to give me my space!" He responded, "Something told me where you would be." This "something" was beginning to irritate Mary-Ann and made her feel like he was watching her in a sinister way. She got in his car and talked to him for a while. She told him that she could not talk to him anymore and she didn't know why, but she couldn't. It was like scales were removed from her eyes when she saw the repeated cycles that kept happening in her life. She was tired of the back and forth and wanted freedom.

She sought counsel from a friend, named Grace, who would advise her that she made the right decision to choose her and to not go back, even if she wanted to. Mary-Ann had never really been alone before. She always had someone to talk to and this was the first time she stopped to look herself. She was abused, broken, and in denial. "How long have I been like this?" she questioned, as she did some self-reflecting. Over the course of a few months, things got better as she continued to speak with Grace about the questions she had. Also, she was growing in her understanding of who she was and the power she had when she spoke. Grace was the first-person Mary-Ann had ever truly let in, and it was scary but, as she removed each arrow, she began to see the wounds from her past hurt.

It was May and the semester was over. It was time to go back home. She was without community, which made her nervous because she did not have any godly friends back home. She only had herself to hold accountable. She stayed glued to her laptop, watching sermons. Her mind was busy, but she was focused. It had been four months since she had intentionally abstained from anything sexual, alcohol, and smoking, and she was proud of herself. She was beginning to adjust to new life, but she began to feel a little weird in her walk of faith around the ending of June and the beginning of July. She did not know what was wrong. Maybe everything was going too great and she could feel something about to happen, but what?

It was the second week in July when she had gotten a call from her father that her grandfather passed away. Earlier that year, she had prayed to God that He would keep her grandfather until July so she could see him, because she knew he was sick, and he was the only grandfather she had left. When she got the call, she immediately was struck with guilt and blamed herself. "Maybe I should've been specific with how I wanted to see him," she cried. She went to her father's house and fell to her knees as she wailed, "I'm sorry, Daddy. I'm so sorry, Daddy." She had never been to either of her parents' homelands, and this would be an opportunity she could, so she agreed to go in place of her father to represent him. She cried for weeks straight as she tried to make sense of it all. That same week, she was scheduled for a flight to Georgia to visit some of her mother's family. She did not enjoy her trip because she spent it crying mostly. With never experiencing a death in her family, she didn't know how to cope with her emotions. One morning, while in Georgia, she spoke to her elder cousin, who is a pastor, and they spoke about Mary-Ann's walk with God. Her cousin told her that God had something in store for her, that he wanted to use her. "But, how?" she questioned. "What do I have to offer to God?" She accepted what her cousin said and just tried to figure out what exactly she could do for Him.

As she went back home, she prepared for her trip to her father's homeland, and the day for departure had finally come. She was excited, but also afraid. She had never been there, but she was excited to see her extended family. Mary-Ann struggled with her cultural identity because she was always told she was too American for the Caribbeans and Africans, and she was too African and Caribbean for the Americans. How do you fit into a society that says you are not enough? There never seemed to be a place for people like her. No matter how she tried to place herself, it was obvious she did not belong. While in her father's homeland, she enjoyed the beginning portion of her trip, as she saw her grandmother for the first time in 19 years. She saw her when she was a baby, but she did not remember. There were not many female cousins, just a lot of males, which made her uncomfortable. She told her aunt, whom she came with, that she would not feel comfortable being alone with any of them because she did not know them, and she did not like being around too many guys. Mary-Ann felt alone while being there. She did not know anyone and did not have a strong relationship with her aunt and uncle that she went with, but she stuck with them most of the time. Mary-Ann had made a promise to herself that, in addition to not having sex, she wasn't going to drink alcohol anymore. She had been underage drinking since she was between the ages of 11 and 12 so, while being on this trip, she promised herself to not touch any alcohol. She was given a "juice" that was really alcohol, and she jumped as the once familiar flavor tickled her taste buds. After the first sip, it was one of the many alcoholic drinks she had while there. Initially, she felt bad but, because of a lack of accountability, she continued to drink. As she drew closer to the familiar comforts, it pushed her away from God, and maybe this was the weird feeling she was feeling in June. The day of her grandfather's funeral had come and gone. She read her father's letter, addressed to his father, in front of the congregation, and she was assigned to read the scripture. How ironic. She had not even prayed or talked to God while she was there, and they chose her to read the scripture? God always has a funny way of reminding us that we cannot escape from Him, but let's see how the rest of the evening plays out. Mary-Ann was given the cold shoulder by her male cousins. They did not utter a word to her the whole time she was there, until after she spoke at her grandfather's funeral. They later invited her to come over for all the cousins to hang out, and she wanted to so she could spend time with her grandmother also. Since they were now speaking to her, she decided it should be fun to hang with the younger crowd for once. She was going to be leaving the country soon, so Mary-Ann asked her aunt for permission, and she reminded her of what she said about feeling uncomfortable. Mary-Ann rebutted that she was comfortable being with one of the cousins she met, thus she was permitted to go, but not until her uncle gave her a lecture on how to behave. He told her, "Be a good girl and behave like a "lady." Respect yourself and, if you feel uncomfortable, call me on WhatsApp at any time and I will come and get you." What did all that mean anyway? She was only going with family members, not strangers, right?

As the day turned to night, July 29, 2019 forever had a shadow casting over it. She was gaining her voice, but that night forever silenced her. There were other neighborhood friends there, so they brought out the drinks, and she was mixing everything with anything she could get her hands on. One cousin, in particular, was acting a little strange towards her. He looked at her and said, "You look like a freak." Puzzled, she questioned, "What?" He asked her if she was a virgin and she replied, "No." He asked her more questions, but what was it to him, and why was he so curious? She disregarded it and began to dance. As she danced, she was breathing again, and she felt at home. She felt alive, but she had intentionally decided to not go back to the old rhythms that used to control her. However, when she heard the beat, her waist moved without her permission. As she danced, her cousin came up and whined behind her. She froze but, on the outside, she continued to smile as if nothing was the matter. "Maybe this is normal," she thought. "Maybe this is what they do." After what felt like an eternity, he left her alone for a little while. The group of kids walked down the road, and Mary-Ann sat on the balcony of a house to wait for her cousins. Suddenly, her cousin approached her, and he began to pull down her dress and kiss at her breast. She pushed him away, but it seemed like her pushback was an invitation for him to apply pressure. As they walked back to her grandmother's place, things started to get a little foggy for Mary-Ann, as the drinks started to go to her head. She did not remember how she got up the stairs but, when she looked up, everyone had disappeared, and she realized that she was now alone with her cousin on the balcony of her grandmother's house. It was dark, and the moonlight was the only light that shined as she wondered where everyone went. He spoke to her, but she could not make out what he was saying. He began to caress her thigh, and then he forced his cigarette scented tongue in her mouth. She stood still as her body went into shock. He brought her down from the balcony and led her into the bathroom. Her body was in full submission to his words. In the dark room, he forced his hands under her black dress as he tore the barrier between her and the world. She stood frozen as he forcibly entered his fingers and touched her soul. He commented on the lubrications and smirked, "You are wet, baby." She had no response except stillness. Removing his hand, she fought to pull her dress down so she could leave, but he held her arms and took what every man has always wanted from her. She covered her mouth and died. "How could this be happening to me right now?" Some of her cousins came looking for her, but her rapist silenced her so she would not be found, and so he could finish. There had now became a disconnection between her body and her mind as she froze and became numb. Her body did not feel like hers anymore, only just a piece of property that was under her abuser's name for the moment. Everything became black as he continued to beat at her soul. She gained consciousness whenever there was an arousal or an orgasm, but shortly after everything went back to black.

So, no one could find her, he took her to her grandmother's room and continued to please himself. She said things to make him hurry up and get off of her as part of the act, but he just went even harder. Then there was a knock at the door. It was her aunt Ria. Thinking she was free, she turned on her side and prayed she would drag him away from her, but he hid behind the door. Her aunt Ria whispered to her rapist, "Leave her, let her sleep." Despite her praying that he would leave her alone, he just came back and took more. He requested, "Don't tell your father, please." She let him take everything he wanted because, from the neck down, she was dead, and she had no feeling. He took her outside, under a light pole to suck her breast and caress himself. Finally, he took her back to the bathroom where it all began. The purity that she worked hard for was snatched from her as he finished and told her, "Go to sleep and remember: keep our secret. Don't tell your father or anyone." As she walked back to her grandmother's room, her cousin, whom she was comfortable with, waited up for her. She smirked at him to make it seem like she was okay but, as she laid on her grandmother's bed, looking at the ceiling, she asked, "You ever feel good for one thing?" He nodded his head, "Yeah". They laid in silence as the summer breeze blew through the room's windows. He knew something happened to her, but she said nothing, and neither did he. She laid on her side and covered her mouth as tears soaked the pillowcase and wondered how she could sleep in the same bed she was raped in. The next day, all eyes were on Mary-Ann, and no one said anything to her. It was like everyone knew that she had been preyed on, like they all knew her abuser was a predator. Her rapist said nothing to her, and it infuriated her. He talked to everyone around her but her. He would not even look her in her eyes and, when he did, he looked at her with much disgust, like she was the scum underneath his feet. One of her cousins, who had come looking for her the night before, pulled her to the side and asked her, "What did he do to you? Mary-Ann, I know he did something. Tell me." She could not tell him that she was sexually assaulted because she was still processing it, and she did not know him nor trust him enough to tell him anything. Her heart was racing, and she could tell everyone was talking about her. She lost it and cursed out her rapist, along with anyone who tried to calm her down. Her uncle, her rapist's father, was passing by and everyone told her to be quiet, but she increased her voice more. Her uncle began to talk to her and ask her what was wrong, but she began to curse him too. He turned to his son, her rapist, and asked him, "What did you do to her? Her vibes weren't like this yesterday, so what happened? As the venom came out of her, she saw the eyes of foreigners, of men she had not known. Quickly realizing this behavior would get back to her father, she apologized to everyone so they would not tell. She went to her uncle and begged him not to tell her father. She apologized, and he promised not to tell her father about her behavior. She did not want her father to question her because, then, she would have to tell him what happened to her, about how she was raped, and how what she desperately wanted was stolen from her— her purity. "Would he even believe me?" she asked herself. "He didn't, when I was 13 years old, when I told him about his friend, because he still allowed him to come around. Why would he believe me, now that I'm 19 years old, about his nephew?"

    To clear her tracks, she invited her rapist to come to the beach with her, her aunt, her uncle, and their cousin, whom she was comfortable with, so everyone would forget what happened that morning. During their time at the beach, she wanted to talk to him about why he raped her, but he convinced her that she wanted it and enjoyed it. While they were talking, he entered into his marked territory. His forcibleness left her hurting but, to not show the pain, she smiled and pretended everything was okay. She stood still and tried to resist the game he played with her soul, but she fell weak and laid vulnerable once again. Mary-Ann had been abstaining from sex but, the more he broke at her soul, the more she desired sex to cover up this confusion she was feeling. He saw that she was confused and afraid, he manipulated her and continued to take what he wanted. As they came back from the beach, she went back to her grandmother's house to say goodbye to everyone and to drop off her rapist. She went to the room he was in to say goodbye to him. She kissed him and grabbed his penis without even thinking. It was not something she wanted to do, but she felt obligated to continue to please him amid her confusion because that was the only thing she knew how to do—please men. He convinced her that she wanted to be rape and that it was consensual. He sold her a reality, and she lived it. She blamed herself for being raped and for the confusion in her mind because she didn't know if she could call it rape since she stopped fighting and froze, kept communicating with him, and continued to give him what he wanted. "Was I really raped if I still talk to him like nothing happened? Is it rape if my body craves more sex, even though it hurts me?" Mary-Ann thought. "Maybe if I start having sex again, it'll cover it up, and I won't think about it because it was my fault, right?" She had no one else to talk to when she was back home and, because her rapist was the only one who knew, she felt she could only talk to him about her confusion. She was embarrassed and hated how, even when they were in two different countries, he still had control over her body. He video-chatted with her and, whatever of hers he wanted to see, she showed him because, if she did not, she felt he would leave her alone to clean up the mess she did not create or tell someone what he did to her. He kept telling her, "Please, do not say anything to your father. I really want to come to Texas, and he said he would help me with that. Don't mess this up for me baby, okay?" She was afraid to speak up because she did not know if anyone would believe her or if he had any pictures of her from the video chat. How could she say anything if there was evidence against her? She felt betrayed by her body because it lubricated from the penetration. She felt it was the reason he did not stop and why he kept saying she liked it, although she did not. Her body responded without her permission and, because of it, she was raped.

While back home in the States, she needed something to distract her from the rape, she went back to the normal things that always distracted her from her pain: drugs, alcohol, and sex. She was told that her cousin/rapist was not the only one who was looking at her, that many of the other men in her family stated they wished they were not related to Mary-Ann. As she heard those things, her heart began to beat out of her chest. If other men were saying this, she thought to herself, then maybe she wasn't crazy and thought she was, indeed, raped. She had to release the weight of the pain, but she was soon to regret it as she confided in her aunt, her father's baby sister. She hadn't opened up to anyone about the rape and the first person she did tell said, "It's your fault. You don't know how to handle your liquor." She went on to tell her, "Anyone you could've slept with, and you chose him? No, Mary-Ann, you have to do better. What will the family say about you? We were all so proud of you." Her aunt claimed to be a woman who was for women empowerment, but how is that when she told a woman, who was raped, it was her fault because of alcohol? Her aunt asked her not to tell her father that she knew because he'd kill her if he knew Mary-Ann was raped, and also if her aunt knew who raped her. She felt like she was protecting everyone while her back was exposed to the world. Hearing her aunt say it was her fault made her feel worthless. She had already believed it, but to hear it out loud just pushed her deeper into guilt and into her coping mechanisms. She never wanted to go back to her father's country, Saint Lucia. In fact, she hated all of his family, especially his sister, who told her it was her fault. She couldn't even look her father in the eye anymore, without thinking about what was stolen from her. She felt defeated because she had been abstaining from sex, and she was beginning to feel pure and holy. All of that was snatch from under her feet. She wondered how God could want anything to do with her now. Consequently, she continued to sink in the hole that was dug for her. To clear her head, Mary-Ann went to a club to dance with a stranger and get drunk. It was familiar, but it didn't feel the same. She had The Waist King blocked for five months and unblocked him because she was lonely. He was in Congo for the summer and she enjoyed talking to him. They caught up, and then he asked her about the two of them. She knew nothing was going to be rekindled between them, she told him politely, "I just need to figure myself out. I do not want to bleed on anyone else." A week after the rape, she saw Leon again, and she felt like he was her saving grace, her saviour from the traumatic reality of life. When she saw him, he looked sinfully fine. He had grown up to be such a handsome young man, but something was odd about him. She asked him, "Are you high?" He laughed, "Can you tell? That was from earlier." Her heart broke. She blamed herself for him going back to drugs. "This is my fault!" she sighed to herself. "I should've stayed with him. He wouldn't have starting smoking again." She did not make any comment about it to him. She just needed an escape for a while, so him smoking again was not a problem anymore. As long as he was back, that's all that mattered.

She was supposed to spend the night with her little sister at her father's, but she wanted to be with Leon. She dropped her car off at her father's, and Leon picked her up and drove her back to his parents' house. The ride was sweet. They looked at each other as the little kids who grew up. Mary-Ann always knew he would come back to her, and she was glad that now was the moment. When they got to his parents' house, she was greeted like she had never left the family. She was excited to see his mother when she went to hug her, and she complimented her on how beautifully she had grown up. Her heart was happy to be received by her old family again because she missed them very much, and they made her forget about all that had happened to her. Leon and Mary-Ann smoked together and, afterwards, they had sex. She was in pain because of the rape, but she didn't say anything. Afterwards, she asked him to drop her back at her dad's. He did but, on the car ride home, he asked if he could take her on a date, and she accepted the offer. She was consumed with regret because they had sex the first night they saw each other again. She needed a place for safety from her pain, but this was just further confusing her already disoriented mind. When he dropped her off at her father's house, she asked, "What are we doing?" He responded, "Let's just go with the flow and see where things go." She looked at him like he was a fool, "I'm not a 'go with the flow' type of girl," she corrected. "You know me!" The next day, they went to dinner and she wasn't feeling him as much. He was excited to see her, but she wasn't as excited anymore. Something about this wasn't right and she knew it, but she couldn't go to God about it because she hadn't spoken to Him in two weeks, which was a long time. She felt like she lost her right to speak to God, so she didn't. She just sat there on the date and soaked everything in. After dinner, they went to a park to chill underneath the stars. She rested in his arms as they looked at the sky. She began to talk about the Ephesians 5 man, and it shocked her because she hadn't spoken to God or read her bible. Why was she talking about the Ephesians 5 man? Leon had no understanding of what she was talking about and she could tell. It was disappointing that he wasn't in his word like he should have been, but what did she expect?

They stayed at the park for a while, then they left to go back to his house. She had this strong feeling to go home, but she couldn't open her mouth to say it. It was like something was holding her mouth and restricting her from speaking. He asked her if she wanted to smoke and she did not want to, but she said yes even though she meant no. Her life flashed before her eyes after taking a couple of hits of the blunt. She began to see a digital clock counting down and her spirit leaving her body. Leon tried his best to calm her down, but she knew it wasn't him she needed. She needed to speak to God because something wasn't right. She tried to sing some worship songs she knew, but her mouth wouldn't open, so she hummed them instead. However, it wasn't enough, so she played a worship song on her phone and began to come down from the high. As she sobered up, she asked Leon to take her home. He wasn't the man she was supposed to be with and she knew it. She ran to many things for safety, only for them place a bridle on her to control her and keep her in bondage. Enough was enough, freedom was long overdue, and she was ready to be free.

8.

Freedom

Mary-Ann had tried everything to fill her void, but they all just added more weight to her sinking ship. She tried men, alcohol, drugs, but nothing worked, and she was tired of going in cycles. The digital clock she saw represented her spiritual life declining and time was running out. No more running or hiding from her pain. It seems like everyone had taken a piece of her, leaving her as a formless being, and it was killing her. She still spoke to Leon after their last time together. She knew she needed to end things, but how? Finally, she blocked his number. He reached out to her on social media and said, "I'm picking up what you're putting down. I'll leave you alone." It broke her heart, but she needed to receive closure from him. She called him and her heart fell to her stomach as she told him, "You are not the man God has for me." As she released those words, she felt a release on the inside of her. It hurt her to tell the guy she had loved since she was 14 years old that they were not meant to be. All her dreams of them ever being together went out the window as she released those words from her lips. As she loosened one bondage, she discovered another. The deterioration of her relationship with her father was the driving force of the void. Leon leaving expanded it, Martin's abuse heightened it, and her cousin raping her exposed it. She was at a dead-end street with nowhere else to run except into The Father's arms, but she was awfully afraid of staining Him with her blood when she removed the arrows exposing where she had been hurt. She had suppressed her emotions for years until it became her identity. Pain and trauma were the things that never changed and, without it, she felt alone. As she stood in the mirror, she couldn't believe the broken reflection she saw staring back at her. "What happened to me? When did it get this bad?" she sniffled to herself.

Mary-Ann's runaway train had come to an emergency halt and she finally had time to take it all in. Her five-year-old self cried out as she screamed for her father. Things were never the same for her when he left. It seemed like life had become a shadow of death when he went away. Her heart never beat with the same rhythm again and her smile wasn't as bright. She had been running for many years because she never wanted to accept that her father's absence was the cause of all this. She didn't want to be another statistic, another young girl with daddy issues who finds love in all the wrong places, but she was that girl and she hated it. She ran from the statistic only for it to stare her in the eyes. She tried extremely hard to be different, to mask her pain through giving herself away, so at least one person could see she was worthy enough to stick around for. She had abandonment issues. When her father left, she put a lock on her heart and when she gave the key to Leon, he used it to play with the seams of her heart after they broke up because he knew he was the only one who had access to her. She laid vulnerable to him because she never forgave herself for the mistake she made when she was 16 years old. She waited for him for four years of her life only to find out that he was not the man she thought he was nor the one she was supposed to be with. It was heartbreaking. She made herself ready for him any time he would come back, but he only wanted what every other man always wanted— just a piece. Everyone had taken their piece, whether it was voluntary or not, and she felt she no longer had ownership of her own body. She was just a tenant renting it. Do you know what it feels like to wake up every morning and take care of a body that is not yours? Or look in the mirror to see a face that has been stained with tears so much that it loses its form because of erosion? She wanted to feel comfortable in her own body and to walk as a free woman, but she never knew she had to expose her darkness to receive the light.

Over the course of the next weeks, Mary-Ann resumed to her first love: writing. She hadn't written in years, and she didn't know where to start. She just let her hands glide across the page.

"I haven't written in you in a while and, boy, do I have a lot tell you. I'm in college now and that's been crazy, but I'm glad to be here…maybe. Life has been crazy, and I do not know where to go or who to talk to. I guess I'll talk to you for now because I know you won't judge me. I'm still very shy and don't speak to people much. I just hold everything in like always. I just wish I didn't have to hold it all inside anymore. I'm starting to feel overwhelmed, and I just want to feel free in my own body. I want to smile without reason and scream from the top of my lungs just so I won't be afraid to speak, but to who? Who would listen to anything I have to say? Would you? I don't know. Maybe I am overthinking like I also do, but whatever. Anyways, enough of that. I am going to bed. I'll update you later."

Unraveling the many layers of the lies that had consumed her, the first one was realizing she was bleeding. Mary-Ann had been running with open wounds, and she attracted many sharks. She hadn't realized that, through her actions, she was crying for a cure from her distress, but no one understood her pleas, so they all mistreated her. As she looked back over her life, she saw the traces of blood and the excess that trailed from her heart. What hurt the most was being young with so much pain. Being only 19-years-old and having to deal with an indescribable pain, she felt stained and unable to ever be pure again. The STD stole her future and her identity, and the rape plundered her righteousness and purity. The second was understanding that she was more than her body, that she had much within her to offer to the world besides her assets. Her father leaving to start other families made her feel like she was not enough. She gave a piece of herself away to men in hopes of proving that she was. She had believed this lie from a young age as people would always compliment her shape and not her face. As she grew up, she became a woman who flaunted her body at men and would wear things that would cater to their satisfaction. Everything she ever did was for them, even if she didn't want to. The label of being a 'man pleaser' was all she knew. It had been repeated to her many times and it had become engraved in her soul. It had become a part of her identity as a woman. She lived by the saying, "Be seen and not heard," as she walked throughout life, but she had much to say. In fact, it was "speak now or forever hold your peace" for her.

    She began to speak up a little bit as she developed a closer relationship with one of the ladies from her church, Chavette. Mary-Ann opened up about her past hurt and how it damaged her self-confidence, value, and strength. As she opened up and released her innermost emotions, she felt weak and vulnerable, like her past was going to be used against her. Mary-Ann didn't understand the power she had whenever she spoke about her pain, and that darkness didn't have to be her abode anymore. She picked up her relationship with God again, and it began to flourish as she became vulnerable with Him more and turned away from the old habits that kept her in bondage. Being vulnerable with God was number one in her gaining her voice back because she had become a silent speaker. She would speak about herself, but never exposed the root of her issues. In the midst of her vulnerability, she questioned what her purpose was in life, and why her suicide attempts at 16 years old didn't work. There had to be a purpose for her existence, but what? She entered college as a biology major because that was the goal everyone had given her, but what were her goals? She went through her old journal and found some of her goals she had jotted down earlier that year. The first one was to become a blogger and create a safe place for people to share their emotions. Expressing herself was something she struggled with because, growing up, she never had the opportunity to feel. She just learned how to roll with the punches life threw at her and, for the first time, she was beginning to feel. It was an awkward and uncomfortable feeling because sharing what was on the inside was not a part of her daily routine and something she had to practice at. This prompted her to change her major to public relations because she always wanted to be an advocate and speak up for others. She always had dreams of writing, speaking, and helping women. As a little girl, she would always record encouraging videos for her future self to look back on. Changing her major brought back many of her dreams, such as starting a blog, becoming an author, having a podcast, and more. She always envisioned herself standing on a stage with a microphone, speaking into a crowd, and it all seemed real and possible. She was beginning to see the keys that would break open the cage so this caged bird could finally sing, but her past kept reminding her of why she wasn't allowed to be free and how undeserving she was of freedom. She never spoke about the rape. She struggled with it in silence, battling in her mind if it were truly her fault, and if she would ever be accepted if she spoke about what happened that night.

This was the first time in a while that Mary-Ann was alone, like completely alone. She decided she wasn't going to talk to or entertain anyone because she wanted to walk without the crutch for once, but the old feelings of needing someone to lean on began to resurface as the past began to play like a broken record in her mind. She was like a baby learning to walk. The first couple of steps are good, but they need support after a while, and so did Mary-Ann. Being completely single was something she was not adjusting to well, and she needed someone to distract her from her reoccurring flashbacks of pain. There was a young man at her church who caught her eye. He had a certain fire in his eyes that made her nervous, which was odd because no man made her this kind of nervous. He was godly and on fire for Christ. She felt she couldn't even step to him because she was rekindling her fire with God. She always viewed God through His relationship with someone else, and she sometimes felt guilt and shame as she would speak to Him. She wanted someone to bridge that gap. She studied the young man from afar and said nothing to him until they were at a bible study and she approached him. This was the most nerve-racking thing she had ever done in her life because she didn't know how to talk to a man without using her body. She told him she just wanted to get to know him better, nothing serious. The two exchanged numbers and decided to meet up the next day. When they met up, he asked her a question that shook her to the core because no man had ever asked her that question. In fact, they really never asked her anything of such substance. He asked her, "What is your story?" and she responded with where she was from and where she went to high school. She asked him to share his story, and she quickly realized he was really asking her how her experiences have formed her into the woman she was. Over the next couple of weeks, he never spoke to her again and it bothered her. "How could he ask such a question and just leave?" she thought. The real issue wasn't about him leaving, but rather she was still trying to use a man to cover up her pain.

As months went on, she realized that she was walking throughout life with a bag filled with pain. She carried it well. Her hunched back felt like she was standing upright. The baggage went everywhere with her. It reminded her of every mistake she made and, if she left the house without it, she'd panic because freedom wasn't something she was used to. She had been in this cage since she was 12 years old and to seek freedom now, at 19 years old, was strange because she always saw life behind a prison bar. Whenever she would pray to God, she would go to Him with her bag and only take out things she deemed important. She never left the bag with Him because it had become her identity, and who would she be if she was totally free? Still suppressing her pain, her 20th birthday came around. She continued to mask everything, hoping no one would notice the cracks, not only in her smile, but in her heart. "God I just want to stop hurting, but it's hard for me to let it go. I'm scared of who I will be without my past because it's all I know and what I can control," she shouted. Freedom isn't free. It always cost you something and, for Mary-Ann, it cost her speaking up.

Mary-Ann had been wanting to start her blog for months but, every time she sat to plan it out, she would create every excuse as to why she couldn't or think herself out of starting, so she never did. Mary-Ann wanted to use the blog as a channel to break her silence and gain her voice to share her testimony with women, letting them know she was abused and broken and how she found freedom. As she did more research on the cost of everything, she was ready to complete the transaction. It was just a matter of pressing confirm, but she wasn't sure. She wasn't sure if she wanted everyone to know the truth about her yet. Did she really have the voice to speak or anything to offer worth listening to? She only told her friend, Grace, that she was thinking of starting a blog, but Mary-Ann purposely missed her original release date, November 22nd, out of fear. To help Mary-Ann reach her new date, December 22nd, Grace gave her an ultimatum. If she didn't publish it by the deadline, Mary-Ann would have to buy her something. That was enough to get the ball rolling for her to start creating, she reached out to a friend named Naomi, who was into filming, and she suggested Mary-Ann make a promo video for her blog. Being the shy girl she was, Mary-Ann was apprehensive at first, but she gave into the idea and completed the video. When it was time to upload it to her social media account, she was nervous. Everyone was going to see and hear her speak for the first time and she wondered, "What would they think?" Excitement flowed from her gentle voice as she posted the video. For the next couple of weeks, she continued to build up her website and, as the deadline got closer, the faster her heart would beat. She could feel herself opening up a little more, and she was beginning to see pass the prison bars. The bridle of fear was losing its grip over her, and it was a weird feeling because she never had power over her own words or emotions. There was a growing amount of confidence overwhelming her, but where was it coming from?

Her first blog post was published, and there was a moment for her to breathe. She didn't know this was the third level to her freedom—publishing—but the fourth level was understanding her testimony before sharing it to the world. She began to ask herself, "Why don't you speak and who took your voice?" As she looked back, she saw her four-year-old self standing on the gated bars of her backdoor, watching her parents scream at each other as her pleas for them to stop escaped from them like a vapor. She saw her seven-year-old self sitting at the table writing as the little boy screamed, "He's not your daddy," and her 12-year-old self crying when her father started another family. Rejection presented the cage, but the abuse locked it. She never forgave herself for what she did to Leon. She blamed herself for ruining her one shot at love, so every other man that presented themselves to her, she dealt with. Her voice faded away as she began to drink and smoke. She never knew how to express herself, so she would release her pain through distractions. The STD stole every thought she ever had of getting it right and finding "the one." It stole her right to choose who she wanted to be with, leaving her to settle for any man who would accept her, so she played the cards she was dealt. The rape made her feel without form, like a woman of no value. All her life, she had been sexualized because of her shape, and to be raped by her cousin justified her worthlessness. It wasn't just outsiders who saw her as just a piece, but those who were close to her as well. It took Mary-Ann some time to understand that what happened to her was rape. She felt that it couldn't be classified as rape since she didn't fight back and she became numb. She felt that her vulnerability left her open to manipulation, which allowed for her rapist to still have access to her and take what he wanted. She felt it was her fault because of the increased sex drive she had gotten after the rape. She continued to give him what he wanted, even while being out of the country, and she felt no one would believe her because she didn't stay away and continued to communicate. There was still a part of her that sought validation from men as she wore clothes that would make her stand out. This burning desire to be seen by men only exposed the emptiness she felt inside. Being alone made her feel undeserving and like something was wrong. She craved for an extra soul just so she didn't have to look at her own. She gave herself permission to take back ownership of her body as she stood in the mirror one day and exclaimed, "You are the owner of this body. You don't have to dress for them anymore." Mary-Ann then threw away the black dress she was raped in and anything else she had one on the trip because it reminded her of her weakness and how vulnerable she was. It was liberating, but only the beginning.

Slowly, but surely, as she talked to God, she began to let go of the bag, no longer taking out a few issues, but now giving Him all of her issues. She felt comfortable being fully vulnerable with Him about her pain, and she allowed Him to see the true version the world could never see. She had been hiding her scars with the color correctors of life just to appear flawless, but the truth was she was tired of applying coverage and just wanted to walk out bare faced in the fullness of her scars. As she spoke with Him in private, her confidence ignited to speak in public because she realized she wasn't the only woman who had been correcting. After starting her blog, things began to change for her as she went from being this shy girl to this bold woman standing in all of her scars and having them on display for the world to see. As she walked in her authority, the foundations of the earth shook underneath her feet, making way for every untouched ground she was to tread. Mary-Ann was no longer seeking validation from men, but she now sought approval from God. Her attention diverted as she focused more on the internal than external. Her outward appearance began to shift as she realized having a nice body wasn't enough to solidify her as a woman or attract the man she needed. Mary-Ann had many great qualities about herself, and she wanted the world to hear what she had been withholding. One of those great qualities was speaking. She had an opportunity to preach the word of God at her church, and it seemed like her life had changed rapidly. "Me? He's really using me? After everything I've done?" She repeated those words over to herself until it finally hit her that God can use anything and anyone for His purpose. Mary-Ann began to lead her church in corporate prayer every Sunday and, before she would begin prayer, her heart would smile with much gratitude. It was the first time she had ever felt real peace.

Being in commune with God was the thing that changed her life, and she was willing to serve Him wherever He called her. She became the president of an organization on her campus that is founded on helping college-aged women walk boldly and freely in who God had called them to be. Mary-Ann saw the position as an opportunity to serve these women who may have been rejected, silenced, or abused. She wanted to share her story with these women to show that the storms always come to yield forth the fruit in you. If she never felt the pressure, she wouldn't have produced. Mary-Ann had gotten comfortable with speaking, you couldn't silence her. This caged bird was finally free, and it was her mission to sing about her freedom. There was a new song in her heart, a new rhythm in her step, and a glow casting on her face. Her smile was genuine and rich. She stood with her head held high and her shoulders back. Every step she took was in confidence and nothing could hold her back. The past began to die as she spoke because she finally realized her silence gave it power.

One the road to freedom, there is always a fight, and the fight reveals how bad you want it. Mary-Ann hadn't discussed much of her rape to anyone and the thoughts soon began to trouble her. She had an increase in triggers that she hadn't realized until she confirmed with herself that she was raped. Seeing her aunt was a major trigger for her. She hated seeing this woman enjoy life while she felt so much pain in silence. Hearing Lucian music was also a trigger, and seeing her father also made her uncomfortable. She was uncomfortable because she lived a lie as she told him she was fine when, really, she wanted to jump in his arms and tell him that his nephew raped her. She wanted to tell him how alone and naked she felt. Mary-Ann didn't know how to feel. Realizing she was raped brought a plethora of emotions and, to avoid them, she drove herself into her work. With much unsaid emotion, she put much stress on her body as she distracted herself in productive work. She did not listen to her body until she was diagnosed with Bell's Palsy. The right side of her face was paralyzed, and her pretty smile was gone. It was at that moment that Mary-Ann broke. She felt like she had no control since being raped. Whenever emotions would come to her, she would go numb because she felt she had no right to feel. She blamed herself for everything. Looking back at the rape, she felt she should've noticed the signs. The signs were clear, his motives were clear, but she was clouded because she let her guard down. She did not want to think about it anymore. Mary-Ann told herself many times, "I should be over this by now. Just get over it already!" But the truth was, she could not because no one knew the truth about her pain, and it crushed her. It hadn't even been a year since the rape, and Mary-Ann just wanted to move on. She had to realize that healing looks different for everyone and healing is a marathon, not a race. She questioned if she could voice her story because it did not reflect the other rape victims' stories she had heard. She was mostly afraid of being judged and misunderstood. She needed to understand that her reaction did not change the action, and how she chose to deal with the rape was her choice. She also needed to know that the increase sex drive stemmed from the trauma. For years, she had paired sex and trauma together. When she felt trauma, she ran to sex. However, in this case, it felt different because she was confused. She did not want people to think it was some incest relationship or that she enjoyed it. She had no control over her body, but would people really understand that?

To push back the thoughts, she continued to blog, and she began to speak live on her social media platforms to connect and reach women all over the globe. Hearing their stories empowered her to keep speaking because someone needed to hear her. Someone needed to know they weren't alone in their pain and that God doesn't look at them differently. Mary-Ann served women as a spiritual midwife—to help them release their pain while birthing their purpose.

Mary-Ann had been trusting God for a healing from the herpes she had gotten from Martin. When she first got her results, she prayed about it and told God she wasn't going to live with the disease for the rest of her life. In that same prayer, He responded and told her, "I'll heal you, but it'll be in my own timing." She didn't think about it again. In fact, she forgot about it, but any time she would say she had herpes, she felt no connection to the disease. It was almost as if she didn't have it, like it wasn't attached to her, like the stain was removed and she was spotless. One thing to understand about healing is that it's a faith thing. Mary-Ann told herself she was healed several times, but she didn't finally perceive her healing until she supported it with faith. In obtaining her freedom, Mary-Ann had to first understand that her healing process was a recovery for her and not a lived-out expectation of others. How she healed was not a determining factor up for discussion. The process began with her writing in her journal to release all the emotions she had felt. She then sought godly counsel because she needed someone to help her fight through her pain. She prayed to such an extent, she thought she was getting on God's nerves by coming to Him about the same thing every day. The next step was receiving His forgiveness and forgiving herself. This was a hard task for Mary-Ann because she could not understand how someone could love her despite all her flaws. How was she able to be seen as innocent, even though she was guilty of the crime? Once she received His forgiveness, she cried unending. How could a love be this great, it offers you a second chance at life and sees you as a new creation? Her mind couldn't comprehend this kind of love or the amount of peace it gives. At the final step, she received the keys to the cage and inscribed on it was "speak."

When Mary-Ann had come back from Saint Lucia, she brought back the country's flag to hang inside her car. She brought it because, finally, she had visited one of her parent's homeland. She felt she finally belonged culturally, even if she hated the country. She wanted to show her father that she was embracing her Lucian side and, also, to have that connection to her father. Seeing the flag every day she got into her car was a reminder of a place she never wanted to go back to and where her life was taken. Looking at the flag made her feel uncomfortable as she saw flashbacks of her rape, but she kept it there to show her father they were connected. Seeing Saint Lucia's Pitons was also a major trigger for her. She hated how something so beautiful could never be looked at the same. Finally, Mary-Ann decided she could not deal with having the flag in her car anymore, and she needed freedom from it, so she threw it away. She threw it away in hopes that maybe the flashbacks would disappear. Maybe the rape would just be a terrible nightmare that she could finally wake up from, and maybe life could go back as she knew it. Unfortunately, it was the complete opposite. Mary-Ann began to question the purpose of even saying anything about the rape in the first place. She felt like gaining her freedom was costing her, her peace, and she wanted everything to go back to the way it was before she began to think about the rape. She slowly started to revert back to being silent and, over time, she became mute. Her relationship with God took a hit, and she was having emotional breakdowns every day, at least three times a day. Her relationship with her father began to change. She had resentment in her heart towards him because he couldn't see she was hurting. He did not recognize her behavioral change and how uncomfortable she was since she had come back from Saint Lucia. She knew she needed to tell her father she was raped, but where could she begin? She was not close to him enough to drop such a bomb on him. She loved him, but he was a stranger. The weight of carrying this secret became too much as she witnessed her father communicate with his sister and his family. She wondered, "Would he still communicate with them if he knew the real truth about them?" She didn't trust his family. While in Saint Lucia, it seemed like they had already been discussing and talking about her. While she was there, on the day of her grandfather's funeral and her rape, her aunt Ria told her rapist, "Don't say anything to her or she'll tell her father." Mary-Ann felt that eyes were watching her the whole time she was there and that, anything she did, they would judge. How do you tell your father that his baby sister is a manipulator and a liar? That his nephew is a rapist? And, that you hate the country he so desperately loves? Mary-Ann knew this was the final thing she needed to do. Her secret could make or break her relationship with her father. The thought of everyone knowing about what happened to her made her nauseous, but her freedom depended on it and she was ready.

Mary-Ann could not hold this in her heart anymore. She needed to tell her father, but when? June was the month of Father's Day, and she did not want to ruin his Father's Day. July would be the one-year anniversary of her grandfather's death and her rape. "When is the right time to ever say anything?" she thought. "Would I even be strong enough to tell him about how I feel in July?" She decided to tell him immediately because it was never going to be the right time to say anything. She wrote him a letter so she would not forget any of the details. Mary-Ann invited her father to a park.

It was awkward at first because she was alone with her father, and she did not really have a relationship with him where they could just talk. She began to read the letter to him. She described the events that led up to her rape and how confused she was. Her emotions overwhelmed her as she confessed, "Daddy, your nephew raped me, and your sister said it was my fault." He rushed from the other side of the table to comfort his daughter and told her, "It's not your fault." He apologized for what happened to her, and he wanted to get to the bottom of it. She told her father that she was afraid to speak up because she did not know if her cousin had any photos of her. She was confused and embarrassed. He reassured her that she was in shock and it's okay because she did not expect that to happen to her. He called his sister and told her, "You let me down. Why would you tell my daughter it was her fault? Why didn't you tell me?" His sister started spouting excuses. "Mary-Ann is smart. She should have known better." Mary-Ann's father expressed to his sister that it wasn't a matter of being smart or dumb. It doesn't exclude you from being raped. Hearing her father take her side relieved her. She was beginning to digest the freedom until it finally registered in her mind that she was raped. She cried to her mother and told her that she wanted to speak with a professional to help her express her feelings and to deal with everything in a healthy way. It seemed like every pain that Mary-Ann had bottled up began to be pushed out from her as she began to cry and release a sound from the pit of her stomach. She did not cry often but, whenever she did, it was not about one issue, but a multitude of things. Seeking professional help was scary for her. It made her feel like she didn't trust God and, with her being an African American woman, that she was weak. All those theories and thoughts were false. There is nothing wrong with seeking professional help to talk to someone. It does not mean you're crazy or do not trust God. In fact, Dr. Anita Philips once said, "Prayer is a weapon. Therapy is a strategy."

Mary-Ann was beginning to move forward in this new-found freedom, but she still felt a little unsettled. Her father was not taking the news well as he began to drink more, and it concerned Mary-Ann. She wondered if she screwed everything up. Was this all her fault? She waited until her father was alone, at about 10 p.m., to speak to him because that was the only time she had him to herself. She asked him if he was okay and he responded, "Everyting good. Don't worry yourself." Her father always said that when he wanted to deflect, but she kept pushing. She asked, "Daddy, are you mad with me?" He responded, "No, I'm not mad with you. I just think to myself that this is disgusting. You meet someone for the first time and this is what you do? I met a lot of women in my lifetime, and I never do this nonsense." He continued to confess that he waits until everyone is gone to cry. He did not want to tell anyone, not even his girlfriend. Mary-Ann felt some kind of way about him not telling his girlfriend because it seemed like she was, again, left alone to carry this burden by herself, and everyone goes back to their normal lives. As the time continued to escape from them, her father told her to go to sleep, but she responded, "This is the only time I get to talk to you." He nodded his head and said, "Ah, I see." He continued to say, "Well, now you won't let this happen again because a mistake made twice is not a mistake. Remember that." She looked at him confused but continued to let him talk. He continued, "You made a mistake, just learn from it and move on." She interrupted him, "Why do you keep using this word mistake as if I did something wrong? A mistake implies that I had some part to play into that, so what are you saying?" He was silent and then he rebutted, "Well, now you'll be more watchful, is all I am saying." A golden silence accompanied them as they sat underneath the night fall. She was confused. Was he for her or against her? "Does he believe me or not?" she thought to herself as she walked back to the guest room she was staying in. She planned to stay at her father's until Father's Day because she thought that after telling him, she couldn't just drop such a bomb like that and leave.

After that conversation, the following morning, her uncle, who took her to Saint Lucia, came by. She was frozen. She was embarrassed all over again. He came making small talk with her, but she knew that he knew she told her dad. He just did not bring it up. She wanted to apologize to him for not telling him about the rape sooner, but she did not know this would be the straw that broke the camel's back for her. Before her uncle could leave, she nervously asked, "Can I talk to you before you leave?" She started off by saying, "I am sorry I did not tell you about everything. I was confused and trying to understand it all." He replied, "That's okay. We all make mistakes in life. Let's just move on." This word "mistake" was beginning to really piss Mary-Ann off. Why do they keep using this word? She asked him, "Why do you keep using the word mistake as if I did something?" He replied, "I spoke to him, and I heard his side of the story." "Are you serious right now? I told you someone raped me, and you go and listen to the side of my rapist? What the actual heck!" she thought as she stood in front of her uncle. He proceeded to spew out the lies that her rapist told him. Her rapist concocted a tale that they were in a relationship, and she talked to him for months unending. He stated that Mary-Ann was in love with him and, when he tried to cut things off, she got upset. Tears began to run down Mary-Ann's face as she cried out, "He's lying! He's lying!" Her uncle told her to calm down, that they were only talking, and she did not need to cry. Her uncle insisted on showing her the pictures her rapist sent him, but she begged him not to show her. He told her, "You aren't the only one that is hurting. I sat in my house by myself and cried. My mother passed out and did not know where she was when she heard the news. She almost died, and my sister Ria cried too." Was he trying to guilt trip the victim for being emotional, and blame her for her grandmother almost dying? He kept telling her, "Don't do anything crazy. If you need help, I will gladly spend my last dime to get you to see a psychiatrist." She told him, "I am not going to kill myself, if that's what you're thinking." "Good," He responded. "It'll cause the family too much pain." Whose feelings mattered more, hers or the family's? Her uncle proceeded to say, "If he raped you, why did you go down on him?" Shocked at such a stupid question, she screamed, "I was in the bathroom with him and alone. He could have killed me! What was I supposed to do?" She walked away and her father called to her, "Your uncle is calling you." She stared at her father for what felt like a lifetime, and he got up to go to her uncle. She went into the guest room, turned up the volume on the television, turned on the AC unit in the room, and screamed so no one could hear her. "No, no, no!" she screamed. "I should have never said anything. No! How dare he say that? That's not right!" As Mary-Ann fought to keep a sane mind, she marched out to her uncle and father, and looked at her uncle saying, "You are the reason people do not speak up about being raped, because of people like you." He looked Mary-Ann in her eyes and said, "How can someone rape you, and you go to the beach with them the next day like nothing happened?" Frustrated, Mary-Ann looked to her father in support that he would silence his brother and, when she saw that he just stood there and said nothing, she grab her father by the collar to get him to listen to her as his child, his daughter. "Daddy, he's lying!" she shouted. Without any warning, her father applied all force on her and looked into her eyes as if she was an intruder as he shouted, "Mary-Ann, what the hell is wrong with you?" He continued to push her back into his truck until his brother and girlfriend grabbed him. Mary-Ann's body was shaking more than the Energizer Bunny. "He put his hands on me," she whispered in disbelief. In all her years of living, her father never put his hands on her and, the day she spoke the truth, he decided to. He yelled, "Go! Leave and go to your mother!" Those words gave her a feeling she has always felt in life. In his eyes, she was disposable.

It was now three against one as everyone commanded her to calm down. She began to spit out venom, and it was a flashback of Saint Lucia, as she defended herself against the foreign men. She talked to her father and he threatened to slap her if she continued to speak. She challenged, "Slap me, please, so that I know this family has more than one abuser!" Her mother came and tried to hold her back, but she broke loose from her grip to give one final goodbye to everyone. Before leaving, she walked past her father's truck and kicked a dent in the side. Her father came charging after her, but she left him in the dust as she drove away. She did not know where to go or where she belonged. She felt everything was her fault and that she ruined everything by existing. She did not want to take her life, but she wanted to disappear. It seemed like anything she did was not enough, or it messed everything up. She was embarrassed. "Great, now everyone thinks I am a psychopath," she thought. She sat on a random neighborhood street as she contemplated her life. She felt this Christian thing was not for her because she kept messing up. She went back to being numb and quiet. That night, she unblocked her rapist and sent him a message. He responded the following morning, and she argued with him for three hours. She needed answers. She asked him why he had the pictures of her, and he replied, "I did it to cover my a**." He told her, "If I raped you, then I raped you good and I should have came in your mouth." He threated to send the photos of her that he had, which were screenshots of the video chat that had taken place when she first got back, to her father. Humiliation is not even the word to describe the insurmountable weight she felt. No one believed her because he had evidence that made it seem like it was consensual. She felt her life was over, that she could never move on from this. She needed help with her mental state as her mind began to wonder, and no one seemed to understand her. Mary-Ann scheduled her first appointment with her therapist and was ready to heal and be free from her mental slavery.

As days drew closer to her first appointment, knots began to form in her stomach. She was nervous because she could not afford to hear someone else blame her for the rape. The day had finally come, and she was on the edge of her seat. She hardly slept the night before because she was scared, but also excited to hear the perspective of a professional. She walked down the hallway to get to her therapist's room. She felt like the walls were closing in on her and it was getting harder to breathe. She sat down in the office and her therapist said, "Hello. So, what brings you in today?" Mary-Ann began to tell her therapist about July 29th and how her life has never been the same. She explained how the weight of the world has been on her shoulders as she has held onto this secret to save herself the embarrassment. Her therapist spoke the words that released the last chain over her heart. "I believe you, and I see nothing wrong with how you responded to the trauma." Mary-Ann knew in her heart that she was raped, and her behavior was a result of the trauma, but she needed to hear a professional say it so she did not drive herself insane. She began to educate Mary-Ann on how the body responds to trauma and that, although it seems crazy to the normal person, it is one of the many responses that can occur with a victim.

To hear those words of confirmation, that she was indeed raped and her response to it did not make it consensual, set her mind and heart free. She was ready to continue with the process of getting her life back together with the help of a professional and her friends for support. Continuing with therapy, Mary-Ann was now walking in total freedom. No chains, no bondage, just free as the wind. Some days were hard. She broke down, but with the strategies she léarned from therapy, she was able to keep moving. It was different, life was different. Here was a life of freedom that she had never known she could achieve or that she even deserved. Yet, it was refreshing to understand her life had meaning and that it was valuable. Mary-Ann continued to work on her craft as a blogger and a speaker. Her strength grew by the day as she realized, she had to live so someone didn't die in their pain or regret. So, the world didn't go another day without the solution that one woman held. Her heart was for healing the broken and being a voice for the voiceless, standing in the gap for those who could not fight for themselves, because she knew that familiar feeling all too well. What a beautiful thing it is to witness a woman realize who she is and the weight she carries within her, that she holds all the cards in her hand and the game only begins when she speaks.

Mary-Ann was me, but now I'm free, and this is why The Caged Bird Finally Sings.

Meet the Author

Robyne Henry is currently pursuing her bachelor's degree at the University of North Texas in Denton, where she is majoring in journalism with a concentration in public relations, and double-minoring in business marketing and communication studies. She is the founder and CEO of Robyne Speaks, which is a platform she uses to reach women where they are, and to aid them by being their spiritual midwife—helping them release their pain as they birth their purpose.

She is a blogger, a writer, a content creator and a profound public speaker. She currently has the pleasure of being the president of an exquisite organization on her campus, Faith Filled Women of Christ. This organization is founded on creating a sisterhood for college-aged women who are seeking a fun, judgement-free atmosphere and are looking to serve and worship as one.

When Robyne is not writing, speaking, or creating, she is serving others and her church. She enjoys reading, learning new recipes, and laughing with her girlfriends.

Connect with Robyne Henry

Facebook: @Robynespeaks

Instagram: @Iamrobynehenry, @robynespeaks

Twitter: @IamRobyneHenry

Website: www.robynespeaks.com

Email: robynespeaks@gmail.com

Resources

Seeking help and speaking about your trauma does not make you weak, it signifies your strength and your willingness to find freedom. And, for that, I call you brave and a conqueror. Below I have listed some helpful resources to help enable you to become the best you, you can be.

National Sexual Assault Telephone Hotline:
1-800-656-4673

National Domestic Violence Hotline:
1-800-799-7233

National Suicide Prevention Lifeline:
1-800-273-8255

Help finding a therapist?
https://www.psychologytoday.com/us

"And they overcame him by the blood of the Lamb, and by the word of their testimony..."
Revelation 12:11

Sources

Faith Filled Women of Christ:
@FFW_UNT
Faithfilledwc23@hotmail.com

https://biblehub.com/revelation/12-11.htm

Made in the USA
Columbia, SC
08 October 2020